Wine Country Living

Wine Country Living

VINEYARDS AND HOMES OF NORTHERN CALIFORNIA
AND THE PACIFIC NORTHWEST

LINDA LEIGH PAUL

RIZZOLI
NEW YORK

First published in the United States of America in 2020 by
Rizzoli International Publications, Inc.
300 Park Avenue South
New York, NY 10010
www.rizzoliusa.com

ISBN: 978-0-8478-6095-1
LCCN: 2019956514

Book Design: Lynne Yeamans

Printed and bound in Italy

2020 2021 2022 2023 2024 / 10 9 8 7 6 5 4 3 2 1

FOR ROBERT

"…and I should like to persuade you that Homer describes wine as
sweet in the same way that Catullus describes it as bitter.
Finally, Homer calls it dark perhaps because he is thinking of
a particular wine prized at the time like the wine that is
called *lacrima** today, which is ruby in spite of the fact that it is
pressed from the same grape as Greek [white] wine."

—TORQUATO TASSO, *The Father of the Family*

**The grape in question (whatever it may have been) is referred to both as having produced the
ruby-colored wine called Lacrima Christi and the white wines of the Levant, Romania, and Venice.*

CONTENTS

Prologue

HANG TIME:

The time between flowering and harvest,
when grapes are left on the vine to achieve
physiological ripeness.

FLYING LEAP RESIDENCE & LIQUIDITY WINERY

OWNER: Ian MacDonald
DESIGNER: Ian MacDonald

There is a house surrounded on three sides by cliffs and gullies. Vertical, shear downdrafts and pulse winds are palpable. Its owner, Ian MacDonald, is someone who—although not yet a wingsuit jumper—has the canny ability to go deeply into creative challenges, convert his interest into successes, and share the results. He stands as an exemplar of the sort of keen spirit that it takes to become a winery owner. In other words, to take a flying leap into the unknown.

To begin, MacDonald and two partners purchased 30 acres of old vineyard land in Okanagan Falls in British Columbia's Okanagan Valley in 2008. The intention was to design and build their vision of a high-quality boutique winery that would become an experience-driven destination. The project consumed four years and most of Ian's time as the key design and development figure of the project and, later, as leader of branding and marketing activities. The launch of Liquidity Wines was in 2012. He had been living and operating out of Montreal, where he had founded and run a company called Moving Products, which provided uniforms and sports apparel for personnel at various Olympic games. He toured the world working for the Olympics and during his travels came to believe that the south Okanagan Valley was

RIGHT: Long rows of lavender begin at the hilltop and are flanked by mounds of wild sage all along the 500-foot driveway to the lower flats of the promontory.

one of the most beautiful places on earth that he had ever seen. Luckily, the budding winemaker was able to land a perfect lakeside property in Naramata, only 30 miles from his now-growing Liquidity Wines, which in 2017 produced 5,600 cases of wine from estate-grown grapes and which also includes a bistro and gallery.

MacDonald found he was spending so much time in the Okanagan Valley that he decided to find a spot in the Okanagan where he would design and build a residence for himself. The property he settled on is 8.5 acres with nearly 420 feet of lakefront that now has a dock and a restored boathouse. The land is pie-shaped, running for 1,000 feet on either side up ancient ravines to meet at a place where creeks once flowed. The design of the

project would take the form of three buildings (the most allowed on agricultural lands in the Okanagan wine country) to maximize views and maintain privacy.

Slope stability is a particular challenge where the soil is predominantly composed of silt deposits, and large setbacks from edges of cliffs can affect the impact of dramatic views. To overcome these restrictions and complications, MacDonald worked with geotechnical engineers to determine that the footings of the original small home and attached carport built on the property around 1950 was solid and stable. This set the parameters for the footprint of the lower floor. The great room on the main floor is comprised of a series of steel I-beams that allow for a cantilever and provide the rigidity and sheer strength to permit numerous

OPPOSITE: Bedroom portion of the studio/guest suite cantilevered out over the ravine.

RIGHT: The wine cellar, on the lower level of the main house.

LOWER: Boathouse and dock on Okanagan Lake.

west-facing windows. The small guesthouse/studio proved more challenging: one third of the 42-foot-long structure is cantilevered over the edge of the south-side ravine, a drop of nearly 200 feet. This is the bedroom area and provides spectacular sightlines, with views of the eroded cliffs and lake that are rarely experienced.

The entire house is set on two massive steel beams set atop four 30-inch-wide holes that were cored down 46 feet deep. Rebar cages were then lowered in and filled with concrete. "No trees were removed or cut down during the construction, and we preserved all of the ancient sagebrush that surrounds the property and lines the 400-foot-long driveway," recounts MacDonald. "Because parts of the main house are only 10 feet from the edge of one cliff, the studio hangs over one of the other cliffs, I chose to call the property Flying Leap. I tell my guests that it is best not to wander off at night. Our goal is [to retain] the protective spirit of this place."

PREVIOUS PAGES: The great room, with 14-foot-high ceilings and a magnificent 42-foot glass wall, offers views both north and south along a 60-mile stretch of Okanagan Lake.

LEFT: In the kitchen, the custom cabinetry is by Meson's, and the molded aluminum laounge chairs with walnut legs are by Baxter, both based in Italy. The custom light fixture is by Alex Beim of Tangible Interaction Design.

ABOVE: Master bedroom in the main house. View looking north up Okanagan Lake. The bed is by Baxter of Italy. The charcoal abstract above the bed is by artist Vaughn Neville.

ABOVE: A panoramic south-facing
view from the tasting room and bistro
complex at the Liquidity winery, which
overlooks vineyards and Vaseux Lake.
A series of Martha Sturdy steel sculptures
plays against the sun and the rugged
vastness of the land.

FOLLOWING PAGES:
Liquidity tasting room. The painting
is by artist Jeff Burgess.

PART I

Introduction

————

"...it is...fundamentally misleading to describe wine
as an *expression* of the soil. It stands to the soil as a
church spire stands to the village beneath it:
a *reaching out* towards a meaning which it acquires
only if we have the culture and faith to provide it."

—ROGER SCRUTON, *I Drink Therefore I Am*

COLE FARMHOUSE
AND SCHOOLHOUSE

OWNERS: Jason and Kisha Itkin

ARCHITECT: Richard Beard, BAR Architects

The Cole House restoration was part of a larger project to
restore an established yet rundown vineyard and winery in one
of California's most distinctive viticultural areas. The land was
cleared of all but the useful structures, including the original
house (probably c. 1860 and called the Schoolhouse because of
the bell cupola on the roof), along with the buildings built by
Dr. R. Beverly Cole and his family—the Cole House and the Old
Barn. The vines were planted and growing long before Dr. Cole,
a prominent San Francisco physician (one of the founders of the
medical school at the University of California, Berkeley), built the
new house and barn in 1889. The property had been purchased
as a weekend retreat, a respite from the foggy climate and social
pressures of the city.

   The Cole farm flourished: oranges, figs, lemons, olives,
clusters of florals, persimmons, copses of fir here and there, and
grapevines all surrounded the well-designed and well-built residence. The property was sold to the Graeser family in 1958 after
70 years in the Cole family. Producing and selling wine continued
on the property until as recently as 2012. The house is located
on a hilly 40-acre vineyard and winery site in the hills on the
westernmost side of Napa County, overlooking Mount Saint
Helena to the north.

RIGHT: The restored Cole House and adjacent Schoolhouse flank a newly
landscaped court from which the owners and their visitors can view the original
vineyard. The old climbing rose in front of the Schoolhouse was carefully preserved
during construction.

LEFT: The wraparound porch was extensively restored, including segments of its Greek Revival railing, and is furnished with a nineteenth-century wood-and-iron bistro bench as well as custom lanterns by Paul Ferrante.

The peaceful isolation of the site and the choice of location within what has become the world-renowned Diamond Mountain District American Viticultural Area inspired the current owners to restore Dr. Cole's retreat as their own and establish Theorem Vineyards there. The restoration of the late nineteenth-century Napa county farm was undertaken when the owners, Kisha and Jason Itkin, a young winemaking couple, contacted architect Richard Beard. The architect's professional eye scanned beyond the overgrown relics of farm life to discern forms of impressive structural elegance. The original 1860s vernacular architecture had been designed to respond to the climate, with its quintessential wraparound porches and deep, comforting overhangs. The floor was elevated to encourage breezes, and tall ceilings facilitate air circulation within the house. The architect kept in mind the significance of the landscape and the buildings, as fine examples of historic Napa County, throughout the project.

ABOVE: Looking south from the new living room, the old cabernet vines are in view. The original Victorian paneling, circa 1880, was reversed and painted, and the windows' original counterweights were exposed. The side table was crafted from an antique millstone.

OPPOSITE: In the main entry are a rare Pierre Lottier bamboo-wrapped iron table with glass top and a rococo secretary, circa 1760. The two-tier chandelier is by Paul Ferrante.

ABOVE: The kitchen, with the main entry and the living room in the background, features a Nero Marquina marble backsplash, dark-leather-and-oak stools, and leather-wrapped stainless steel pendant light fixtures.

RIGHT: The master bedroom features north- and east-facing views of Mount Saint Helena and a custom, iron four-poster bed and custom walnut, bronze, and linen upholstered sofa. The windows retain their original cast glass. Ceilings throughout the house are composed of all new Douglas fir beams and decking.

Following extensive historical research, Beard updated the historic structure but preserved the character of the original design. Extra care was taken to preserve and reuse as much of the existing building materials and structure as possible. The majority of the exterior and interior woodwork was restored, including the window frames and the interior redwood cladding and fir floors. Modern sustainable features include a fully insulated building envelop, new high-efficiency HVAC system, and new plumbing and electrical systems. The restoration of existing passive features of this vernacular house combined with the addition of modern active systems result in a very efficient modern farmhouse.

The qualities of the painterly surrounding landscape can be viewed from almost every window in the house. The restoration had become a picture postcard of a quintessential Victorian-era farmhouse.

PREVIOUS PAGES: From the cabernet vineyards, the full historic compound comes into view at dusk. On the far right is the Cole House, and just to its left is the Schoolhouse. In the foreground is the Long Barn, which served as a commercial chicken coop and is now a garden pergola used for outdoor dinners.

LEFT: In front of entrances to the main house and the Schoolhouse is a new courtyard with a tree canopy.

ABOVE: A picturesque outbuilding at dusk.

JØRGENSEN RESIDENCE

OWNERS: Brandon and Katy Jørgensen

ARCHITECTS: Walter Thomas Brooks (original structure);
Brandon Jørgensen, Atelier Jørgensen

This alluring jewel in the landscape is an homage to the early theories of organic architecture. The 1960 "Petal House," as it was once known, was designed by Walter Thomas Brooks, a California architect who found architectural inspiration, like many before him, in the forms of the natural world. Brooks's ideal of organic architecture focused on the mechanisms that form nature's processes: how an arrangement of purposeful components organize around a singular guiding principle of unity, a principle which appears in the scientific writings of those curious seekers as diverse as Charles Darwin, Walt Whitman, Antoni Gaudí, and Frank Lloyd Wright. The principle of unity and its variations are shared among poets, evolutionists, biologists, even farmers and viticulturists, who understand that for the finest results one must begin with the purest rootstock.

LEFT: View from the bocce ball court up the slope to the main house and grounds.

Brooks's organizing principle followed the evolution of the seed of an organism. The structure of this house is defined by its sweeping petal-like roof, which covers the structure with large overhangs that embrace and protect the terraces. From a distance, the elegant overhangs frame distinctive features of the landscape: gentle mountain and valley views, respites under hovering trees, and a variety of areas of repose and recreation. In 2012, Brandon Jørgensen and his wife, Katy, discovered the house in a state of severe long-standing distress. Still, they understood the underlying perfection and possibilities of the location and the house, which was not on the market but was available to rent. Katy and Brandon moved in, and with their own funds, they slowly began to make improvements. After a few years, the owners could see the love the Jørgensens had for the house and eventually agreed to sell to them.

The Petal House was about to bloom. Pure rootstock is a perfect beginning. However, daily pampering, vision, and hard work is what prepares the rootstock for future grafting. Before the ink was dry, the Jørgensens brought in heavy equipment and began a three-year process of sculpting, rehabilitating, and repairing the land. The work included constructing multiple terraces, quarrying boulders and stone from the property, and adding stairs and paths from the house to the new terraces. A spacious lawn, a regulation-size boccie court, a firepit, a meditation terrace, and a barbecue terrace were all constructed to surround the house. Also added to the property were a copiously productive vegetable and herb garden, citrus and peach trees, and a pond with lilies, frogs, and turtles.

ABOVE: Bocce court under the large old oaks that populate the property.

OPPOSITE: The terrace adjacent to the master suite was designed to accentuate the western angles of sunlight.

LEFT: In the spacious living room, wood-framed doors and windows open to the lush landscaping and a private terrace. The dining room is adjacent to the living room and has views of the valley below.

With a new landscape design on its hillside site, the house now had views of Mount Tamalpais, Mount Veeder, the Napa River, and downtown Napa. The project had been improved tenfold by connecting the house to the landscape so that it would be used year-round. Once attention could be directed back to the house itself, slight structural and cosmetic repairs began. The large overhanging eaves were addressed. In the kitchen, cabinets, surfaces, and appliances were upgraded. Converting a too-small carport into a glass-enclosed library and workspace was a beautiful modification. Bathrooms were gutted, redesigned, and refinished. The house was beginning to show its personality. The work and passion of the Jørgensens over a four- to five-year period achieved on every level the evolution of architecture that Walter Thomas Brooks had only dreamed of: a vernacular structure that could not have been designed or built for any other location.

ABOVE: This wood-clad interior offers a solitary reading room with a classic modern fireplace of vertically stacked brick and concrete. The firepit is built above a concrete bed that runs the full width of the room and is surfaced with a protective layer of gravel.

OPPOSITE: The original carport was converted by Brandon Jørgensen into his first atelier.

TELESIS 2.0

OWNERS: Anonymous

ARCHITECTS: Jack Hillmer (original structure);
Katherine Lambert, MAP Architects

If you did not grow up in California you might look at this house, Telesis 2.0, and think of it as a quintessentially modern, West Coast summer house of the 1950s: the sleek entrance, the parking area just under wide-branched leafy oaks, a swimming pool in the center of a red concrete patio, and a nearby 54-paneled floor-to-ceiling wall of glass nearly enclosing the patio. The roof is folded and delicate—reassuringly asymmetrical, imaginative, necessary—and held aloft with a redwood-posted clerestory running the length of the front half of the house. It is pure California design.

Modernist architecture emerged throughout the forests and valleys of the Napa region during the 1950s at a pace barely noticed in its own time. California buzzed and burst with creativity, with the modernist urge finding expression in well-designed and solidly built weekend getaways. Hundreds, perhaps thousands, of projects were taking shape on seemingly every one-acre parcel, at the end of every dirt road that turned off a country road and progressed up or down through the trees. These hidden treasures often were designed by young architects for young families. Over time they became rentals but then were virtually forgotten, falling into disrepair. Architecture critic Alan Hess writes passionately about the delayed and late discovery of the work of those fine California

RIGHT: This light and airy house is a testament to the spirit of optimism and exuberance that mirrored its moment in California history.

architects whose work went unknown or unrecognized for three or four decades or more. The best examples of these architectural treasures of the era of mid-century design, their best work, eventually began being "discovered" or "uncovered," one at a time.

Telesis 2.0 is one of those rare discoveries. Designed by Jack Hillmer in 1953, the house epitomizes sleek through the use of his preferred materials: stainless steel, glass, concrete, and old-growth redwood, which he employed within his small oeuvre of only ten finished buildings. The residence is as light and airy as it is a testament to the spirit of optimism and exuberance that mirrored that moment of California's collective history.

When Katherine Lambert and Christiane Robbins, partners in MAP Architects, considered the purchase of the house in 2011,

the costs of restoration were a factor. The partners were aware of the historical importance of Hillmer's work. It was only after a consultation with a wood restoration expert who had experience working on the restoration of a Hillmer residence that Lambert and Robbins felt confident enough to begin the project. Lambert and Robbins considered every detail, large and small, and decided that the challenges involved would be worth it in the end. The team then set out to create a more livable space in the house; reinforce the structure; restore the unfinished, old-growth, clear-heart redwood; spend $15,000 to glaze and adapt the glass for the reduction of heat loss; and reconfigure the landscape design and pool with irrigation systems. MAP Architects conserved the original footprint while redesigning and expanding the entry,

OPPOSITE: The residence is constructed of only four materials: unfinished old-growth clear-heart redwood, Basalite blocks and pavers, floor-to-ceiling glass panels, and stainless steel.

RIGHT: A quiet hollow and duck pond.

BELOW: The front entry is under an undulating folded-plate copper roof. Clerestory windows flow above the entrance side of the perimeter walls.

kitchen, and bath spaces and revitalizing the interior circulation to align more closely with twenty-first-century sensibilities.

During the evolution of this classic Hillmer design, the partners were aiming for landmark status with the town of Napa. The architects worked closely with Napa officials to ensure that the significant, detailed design decisions and evolutionary steps they took would not only bring the Jack Hillmer house into the twenty-first century but also get it recognized as a cultural landmark, the first post–WWII residence to be honored as such.

L E F T : The interior is based upon an integrated, expansive counter-clockwise plan spiraling outward from a central tower anchored by a custom-designed, Rumford-style fireplace.

B E L O W : The single-level structure features a custom black-concrete floor.

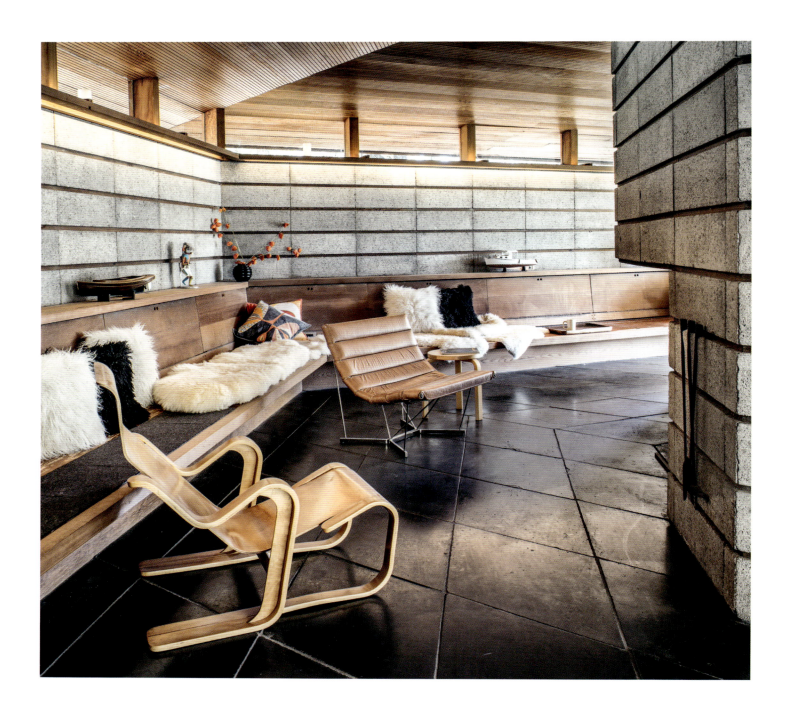

ABOVE: The spiral floor plan
moves through the leisure area, around
the central fireplace.

OPPOSITE: A leisure reading
spot in the quiet stretch of the spiral.

PART II

Sonoma

———

"It is only wine in the way that a Picasso
is only paint on a canvas and that
music by Mozart is only vibrations in the air."

—BIANCA BOSKER, *Cork Dork*

LOVALL VALLEY

OWNERS: Ginger Martin and Fred Favero
ARCHITECT: Conrad L. Asturi Studios

A creek runs the length of lovely Lovall Valley, the coldest place in the region to grow grapes, making it a Region 1 viticultural area. The valley is accessible only from Sonoma, where the mouth of the Lovall Valley is found through the curves of fast, narrow roads and hills and dips covered in thick, live oaks with branches spread wide and lush.

The orientation of Hillside House was designed to gain the benefit of cooler air and breezes and the sweeping views from the northwest, as well as to take advantage of the native broad, thick-branched, shading oaks and indigenous shrubs. The entry to the house is through a series of natural foliage. Multilevel concrete and stucco volumes of planting medium or pools of water are profuse with water-planted papyrus, modernist water rush bamboo, and Mexican fan palms that create a beautiful privacy wall. The front door is flanked by two of the reflecting ponds, which contain sculpture by a local artist. A gallery of stone,

RIGHT: Acres of young vines are just steps away from the house and the barn.

art, concrete inlaid with steel, and carved marble seating bring a mellow coolness to the air and to the entrance of the courtyard. An open plan in the great room has a movable glass wall that opens out to the outdoor living space. Just a step inside, the kitchen area combines a dramatic eucalyptus island with a bar, Carrara-marble-backsplash wall, and limestone counters.

The back of the residence is designed to be the entertainment/ dining area of the house. The owners hold wine tastings around a custom bar and a limestone table that was designed for the space. The outdoor kitchen features everything required for alfresco enjoyment. Once again, wide overhangs become a star architectural feature, creating shaded areas for all guests, whether dining or lounging. This lovely recreational area merges with the lawns and the swimming pool. Additional terraces made of volcanic rock sweep downhill to offer views of Mt. Tamalpais to the south and Sonoma County to the west. The house sits on 24 acres, with 6 acres of vineyards planted in Cabernet Sauvignon and Sangiovese grapes, a winery, and two wine caves. The sloping site toward the southwest also faces the Mayacamas Mountains, which reshape the angles of the afternoon sun into an element of ongoing entertainment and delight. With a glass of wine in hand, guests can enjoy unmatched sunsets at the end of a long day.

OPPOSITE: View of the entrance and library. Recessed windows and architectural overhangs are designed to provide depth as well as shade.

RIGHT: The terrace is a concrete grid with teak inlay. The lounge chairs and table were designed by Alwy Visschedyk.

BELOW: In the entry court, sculptures by Mark Chatterley are mounted above a reflecting pool.

PREVIOUS PAGES: Large concrete overhangs allow sufficient shade to offer protection from the sun and heat.

LEFT: The kitchen island has a blue gum eucalyptus base with corten steel detailing. A custom blackened steel range hood is mounted above a Carrara-marble backsplash.

BELOW: Near the interior entry, a Brigitte McReynolds painting hangs around a corner from a rusted-steel mirror from Mexico.

RIGHT: The dining area of the great room looks out onto a dazzling oak tree.

RIGHT: In the large central room of the house, white linen sofas by Verellen flank both sides of a large blackened-steel media wall with an integrated fireplace. The hemp ottomans and ball pillow are by Wendy Owen Design. The textured mango-wood trunk side table was crafted by Louise Mann.

SONOMA COAST VINEYARD RESIDENCE

OWNERS: Anonymous

ARCHITECT: Cutler Anderson Architects

On clear days, views of the Pacific Ocean are part of the wild and invigorating Sonoma coast. The marine conditions for cultivating grapes are advantageous in many ways: each plot of terroir provides a distinct character to the grapes. Here, the temperatures are the reverse of those at higher elevations: days are cooler and night temperatures are warmer in the 18 American Viticultural Areas of Sonoma County. The Russian River, the maritime breezes, and, of course, the warm comfort of marine fog are a few of the elements that influence the characteristics of the grapes.

The house on this ridge is designed to take advantage of a natural forest's edge that winds behind the structure. Here, the architect begins to play with lightness and darkness. Everything about architecture is the way in which an architect manipulates the available light. It is the allure of design, orientation, angles, and refraction of light. James Cutler utilized the density of the forest to emphasize the lightness of the field—an obvious play on the wholesomeness of untrained nature and the rigid protocols of a viticultural enterprise. The architecture within this complementary partnership should create an emotional connection between the environment and the senses.

LEFT: The house is tucked into the edge of a dense forest where the land rolls away to the vineyards.

The physical experiences of the residence can be found in how one becomes aware of the variations in the ridge itself, the height of the trees, the roof slope of the house, and the sloping of the vineyards themselves. Obvious contrasts are seen in the thick, rammed-earth walls and their reliance on the thick forest of bay and redwood trees against the lightness of the interior wood and the light colors of the walls with the variation in hues. Glass walls, which allow for massive amounts of daylight, play against the solidly anchored exterior of the house to the forest and to the earth. Again, contrast is expressed in the lightweight roofing component, a structure whose graceful lightness is enhanced by beautifully angular clerestory windows that frame the lush upper boughs of the trees. The wood roof and tapered column system

is designed to resist lateral movement while still utilizing the materials at their highest possible dimensions.

Emotional expression of the design begins naturally in the approach to the house through the shaded cool and dark of the trees, found in the continuum between earth and the sky, dark and light. Designed less as an object and more as a series of sensory events, the house puts to rest decades of plans for living that attempted to combine the ideal of an inside-outside architecture. The visual cues that Cutler incorporated into the design of this coastal residence provide discrete experiences of the terrain, the vines, the fog, the ocean and maritime life, the vineyard and farming life and confirm the mesmerizing, absolute necessity of trees. The substantial amount of bright wood used in the interiors

ABOVE: The house and forest are enveloped in fog as it rolls in at dusk.

TOP RIGHT: View of pool looking southeast at dusk.

BOTTOM RIGHT: One enters the house through thick, rammed-earth walls.

reflects the variety of color tones found in the rammed-earth walls. On these walls, the architect went into the formwork and drew, in chalk, where the lines of dark and light earth would appear on the interior wall. This created a gradation from darkness at the bottom to very light and sandy at the top to express the feeling of being at the beach. Jim Cutler and his team understand that the ultimate objective of any architectural design is to reveal what is true about all of the circumstances of a project.

OPPOSITE: The massiveness of the rammed-earth walls throws into relief the lighter nature of the wood.

ABOVE: View of the living room through to the dining room. Tapered columns set into the floors support the roof. On clear days, the living room offers views to the Pacific Ocean.

DRY CREEK RESIDENCE

OWNERS: Anonymous

ARCHITECT: John Maniscalco Architecture

Sonoma County is home to 18 American Viticultural Areas (AVA). Each AVA has its own microclimate, each determined by marine air currents, elevation, angles of the sun, terroir, fog, rain, and wind. Dry Creek Valley is north of, and almost contiguous to, the Russian River Valley. The region is home to the typical coastal topography, with damp, cool valleys and sunny, warm high-elevation hillsides. The growers welcome coastal fog for a cooler-growing grape, while varietals, such as sauvignon blanc, are the most planted white grapes. Sauvignon blanc, originally grown in the Loire Valley in France, where church bells toll in the morning and cowbells sound their way home in the evening, is a crisp, varietal wine with a hint of minerals and vigorous citrus flavors. However, the hills that rise above and beyond the fog are warm and where the grape that Dry Creek Valley has become renowned for, the California Zinfandel, grows.

Above the viticultural treasures of the ever-growing Dry Creek Valley sits a residence designed by John Maniscalco. On a warm and sunny 6.6-acre hillside site above Healdsburg, the nexus of

RIGHT: A seamless connection with the terraces and pool extends the great room spaces perfectly into the courtyard.

Sonoma wine growing, sat a 1970s ranch house. The owners asked Maniscalco to rebuild and expand the structure in a way that would change its relationship to the site and reflect the way the owners lived in the house. The original house had been built above the entry drive and parking spaces, which meant looking over the paved parking area below to take in the scenic vista of romantic hills and colorful sunsets. The entry drive and parking area were relandscaped. The entry was relocated behind the house, with views revealed as guests approach. The house connected to the landscape and became surrounded by it.

The introduction of new linear forms arranged new component areas of the home around a central courtyard to create a family compound that is anchored to the flourishing landscape in an entirely new and breathtaking relationship. Trellised shading treatments connected the individual elements to the new distinct wings, separating the public living areas from the private bedrooms and the guesthouse and garage. The valley floor and the Dry Creek vineyards are visible from every room. Carefully composed, deeply cantilevered overhangs and slatted sun shades manage the rays of the summer sun while allowing the winter sun to penetrate into the interiors. The rich palette of natural materials, including western red cedar siding and concrete flooring, anchor the structure to its natural environment and reinforce the seamless relationship to its surroundings. The beautifully sited infinity pool extends the spatial experience as the centerpiece of the overall composition and mirrors the dramatic skies of Sonoma.

LEFT: Beneath a manzanita tree, a treasured family sculpture watches over the valley below.

ABOVE: A fully glazed entry hall introduces visitors to carefully framed views of the full landscape of the Dry Creek Valley.

BELOW: The entry drive drops into the hillside site, allowing views that hint at the panorama beyond. A slatted cedar-clad volume provides privacy and containment while granting selective views.

PREVIOUS PAGES: Carefully nestled into the mature growth of the hillside, the house has wings that extend into the landscape and frame a central courtyard that modulates the sloping topography.

LEFT: The spaces of the great room flow outward toward the courtyard and pool through retractable doors beneath deep cedar-clad overhangs.

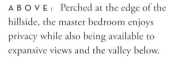 Perched at the edge of the hillside, the master bedroom enjoys privacy while also being available to expansive views and the valley below.

RIGHT: Oversize pocket doors retract into oak-clad cabinetry that reveals a discreetly placed media room adjacent to the living leisure space.

SONOMA VINEYARD ESTATE

OWNERS: Anonymous
ARCHITECT: Aidlin Darling Design

The owners of this lovely Sonoma land sought a quietly monastic home gracefully integrated into the land. Situated at the base of Sonoma Mountain, this 140-acre estate includes a main residence, a guesthouse, a vineyard and vineyard barn, and garden spaces, as well as sculpture gardens and the later addition of 60 acres of vineyards. The buildings are sited within the landscape to support a harmonic coexistence of demanding day-to-day vineyard operations with the ideal of a rural domestic life through a serene expression of the spirit of the place. Each structure is discreetly woven into its unique place in the landscape without any disturbance to the overall panoramic vistas. The site was composed of extremes. Old gnarly vines marched along in rows. Much of the original vineyard perimeter, which required replanting, was bordered by the Sonoma mountainside and breathtaking redwoods. Dominating all was a broad open view spanning the valley, facing eastward to the Mayacamas Mountains.

The house slips quietly onto a narrow rise at the edge of the vineyard to face the valley below. The owners sought a seamless blending of their art collection and furnishings, the buildings, and the landscape. The main residence was designed as a series of

RIGHT: The house sits quietly on a narrow rise at the edge of a completely replanted vineyard facing east to the Mayacamas Mountains.

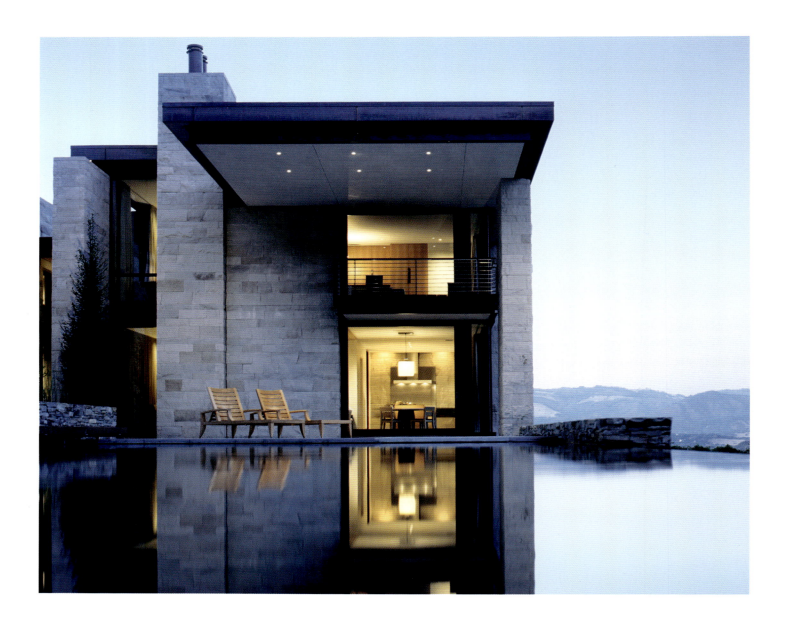

ABOVE: The south-facing living spaces extend onto the pool terrace. The infinity-edge pool overlooks the vineyard and the backdrop of the hills.

OPPOSITE: The north facade of the building, adjacent to the north-south axis of reflecting pool, orients the building into the site.

connected spaces around a loggia and reflecting pool. The linear pool runs along a north-south axis, acting as a primary orientation device among the rolling vine-clad hills. The sequentially ordered interior spaces are individually defined with balanced natural light through well-placed floor-to-ceiling windows amid tall walls for artworks, which appear cinematically while sustaining a perfect orientation with the landscape beyond. The handsome views of the topography were thoughtfully and carefully crafted.

A guesthouse is situated on an existing plateau between the vineyard and the mountain. It is constructed around a central rammed-earth wall that shelters warm interiors on one side and

OPPOSITE: Lighting from the dining hall and the second-floor gallery is reflected in the evening waters of the pool.

RIGHT: The north-south axis of the reflecting pool organizes the geometry of the home and creates the ceremonial space of the dining room.

cool, intimate gardens against the forest on the other. The 18-inch-thick wall is woven among the existing trees and anchors the building structurally, ecologically, and experientially. Floor-to-ceiling glass frames sweeping valley views, while allowing openings to the exterior surrounding terraces. A pathway through the vineyard leads one due east to garden rooms filled with vegetables and lavender. The gateway walls hold a time capsule to be opened on March 21, 2103.

The resulting home is one that is graced with light, exquisite views, and perfect proportions. It is a sculpture that manages effortlessly to be both a home for two and welcoming to relatives, neighbors, and friends. Daily life is centered around cuisine—Sonoma is the source of inspired produce for the table and of superior wines—and the owners enjoy the quiet grace of special family time and the tranquility that ideal proportions create for one's sensibilities.

LEFT, TOP: Narrow portals through the massive stone walls frame layered views of architecture, constructed landscape, agriculture, and nature.

LEFT, BOTTOM: A stone fireplace anchors the sitting room, which overlooks the surrounding gardens.

BELOW: Double-height windows in the living room frame eastward views over the vineyard to the distant mountain ridge.

OPPOSITE: Furniture and accessories that are alternately rustic and zen create an idyllic space for repose.

OPPOSITE: The entry foyer of stone, wood, steel, and glass.

RIGHT: The hallway leading to the bedroom wing doubles as an art gallery.

BELOW: Large steel-and-glass pivot doors connect the dining room to the vineyard.

LUCUNDA VINEYARD RESIDENCE

OWNERS: Anonymous

ARCHITECT: Swatt Miers Architects

Lucunda Vineyards has been producing and selling Pinot Noir grapes to local wineries for 15 years. The property and vineyards were recently purchased by new owners who wished to pursue their plans to become more a part of the wine-making process. After the owners conducted an exhaustive search for vineyard property in France several years ago, their pilgrimage brought them to the winescapes of California and their wine-making dream. It was love at first sight when they glimpsed the spring-green undulations of slopes and knolls and oaks that realized their vision of planting, growing, tasting, harvesting, and producing as part of their active life. They set out to build a modern home that would live in harmony with the working vineyards.

To take full advantage of a spectacular, approximately 20-acre setting in in the Russian River AVA, the heart of wine country, this seemingly effortless blend of architecture and agriculture is sited atop a sloping knoll gracefully encircled by 16 acres of high-quality Pinot Noir vineyards. Fields and hills of vineyards are visible from interior rooms of the house and

RIGHT: Walkway to the entry court from the northwest.

from casual outdoor terraces. The pool area and surrounding landscaped paths lead to shaded areas under heavily boughed oaks, with tables for alfresco lunches.

The house is designed in an elongated T-shaped plan, with two distinct facades that distinguish the business activities from the family living activities. The entrance to the structure is a luxurious composition of volumes, relatively opaque to maintain privacy. The sight lines as well as the natural light are carefully controlled through delicate wood-screened walls. In contrast, the south side of the house is all glass, including glass walls that open the interior spaces to an expansive swimming-pool terrace. The terrace is a retreat from the afternoon sun. The detached

guesthouse sits at the terrace edge as a glass box with 270-degree views of the landscape. A deep floating roof spans the main house and the guesthouse, making a perfect place for a sun-protected outdoor kitchen and dining terrace overlooking the picturesque western and southern vineyards.

The owners' favorite time of day is morning, awakening to the California sunshine over the vineyards or watching the Russian River Valley morning mist roll in. Enjoying a cup of coffee on the terrace with birdsong in the air, one can observe the sun clearing away the morning mist. Whether sun shining or fog misting, mornings at the Lucunda Vineyard residence are a dream come true for this family.

OPPOSITE: View of the entry from the great room. The terrace avails itself of breezes coming through the aged live oaks.

RIGHT: A quiet place for an afternoon drink.

BELOW: The glassed-enclosed guest suite overlooks acres of vineyards through an allée of live oaks.

ABOVE: A path leads from the house to the bocce ball court, which overlooks the vineyards below.

RIGHT AND FOLLOWING PAGES: The easy, elegant essence of the Napa lands and vineyards at mid-afternoon and at dusk.

IRON HORSE VINEYARDS

OWNER: Joy Sterling

Driving up to Iron Horse Vineyards for the first time gives you the feeling of going back a generation or two to a place you already know. The road is a single lane, rutted, with vineyards on the right. The fence line is wild—roses and cultivated flowers grow alongside weeds. You see signs along the fence posts: Slow Down, and a little further, Slower. Then, at the top, it says Enjoy the View. It makes no difference, the atmosphere and air have already taken hold of you. Everything is unassuming, yet it says that someone cares and is *still* caring for this place. And you are happy that you found it.

The view as you near the center of the property features grapevines in the foreground, a tasting room and barns a half mile away on the hill. At the crest of the rustic knoll, Iron Horse impresses as one of Sonoma County's most beautiful small, independent family-owned estate wineries. It is located at a place where the ocean fog flows in the 10 miles from the Pacific coast to settle in the Green Valley AVA, with one of the most distinctive

RIGHT: The Iron Horse vineyards come into view as the old road rounds the rise at the top of a hill.

LEFT: The outdoor tasting area of Iron Horse is the place to enjoy their fine sparkling wines, which is served along with barbecued fresh oysters and cavier on Sundays.

BELOW: The Iron Horse vineyards occupy the highlands of Sonoma County.

RIGHT: The original Iron Horse weathervane.

FOLLOWING PAGES: A cool Sonoma morning on the old road to the top of Iron Horse Vineyards.

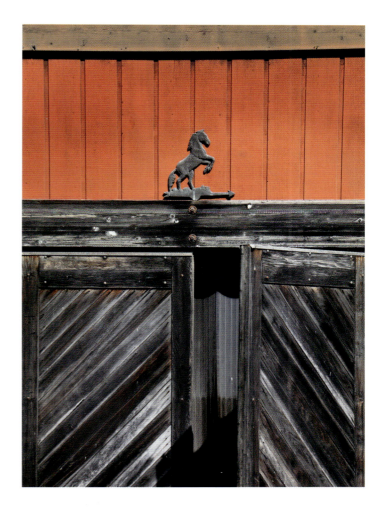

soils of the north coast. The Iron Horse vineyards and its endless gardens of vegetables, fragrant florals, fig and olive trees, as well as rows of palm trees that line the road, breathe character and time. Iron Horse exemplifies the American West Coast dream of making wine. The owners' story shows that no matter your original calling in life, if you are tough, committed, resilient, and a little bit obsessive, you too could have what it takes to be a winemaker.

This story begins in 1976, when Barry Sterling and Audrey Sterling, Joy's parents, bought Iron Horse Vineyards. As early as the 1850s there were farmers in the area who grew small crops of grapes. Three generations later, by 1935, a few farmers had bravely evolved into grape-growers and winemakers. Mid-twentieth century was the most explosive financial and experimental period in California. Farmland slowly transformed into prime vineyard-growing regions.

Audrey gave Barry his first trip to Europe for his thirtieth birthday. He fell in love with France and vowed one day to live there. Eight years later, in 1967, prominent and successful in Los Angeles, they and their two young children, Joy and Laurence, took the leap and moved to Paris. There, they immersed themselves in the French culture. Audrey's table became quite well known in Paris: their Belle Epoque dining room seated 40. Favorite dinner guests were an entertaining mix of former artist's models, admirals, wives of former politicians, bourgeois bankers, magazine writers,

authors, and artists. Barry Sterling adored the large French apartment they lived in, which came with three underground wine cellars, each of which held 5,000 bottles.

Joy's mother and father traveled throughout the wine-making regions, and along the way they became increasingly interested in buying a château. One night, they went to a grand wine tasting in Paris at the three-star Taillevent restaurant. It was a blind tasting for professionals and connoisseurs. Nonetheless, Barry Sterling was the only one who guessed the mystery wine, a Bourgeuil that he had once consumed in vast quantities with Alexander Calder in Calder's studio in the Loire Valley. Sterling recognized it by the way it burned his throat. The next morning, he was written up in the *International Herald Tribune* as one of those rare Americans who bested the famous French tasters. Eventually Iron Horse would also best the French competition. Iron Horse wines are celebrated worldwide, and its sparkling wines, both the cuvées and brut, meet the challenges of the best of France.

SONOMA HILLSIDE HOUSE

OWNERS: Gregory and Kathi Hansen
ARCHITECT: Harvey Sanchez
DESIGNER: Conrad Sanchez

This Lovall Valley house was designed by Harvey Sanchez and his son, Conrad Sanchez, and Edan Asturi. The residence sits atop a steep hillside overlooking the Carneros wine-growing region in Northern California. Sonoma County shares Carneros with Napa Valley, and many vineyards of the Sonoma Valley American Viticultural Area are located within this sub-appellation as well. Nearby San Pablo Bay, at the northern edge of San Francisco Bay, keeps the Carneros a cool and breezy environment. The area's dense clay soils are not particularly deep or fertile but instead very thin and shallow, providing poor drainage and fertility, and make the vines struggle to retain moisture. However, in vintages with a long, drawn-out growing season that allows the grapes to ripen, intense and exceptional flavors can develop. Because it is the coolest and wettest growing region on the coast, it is the first area where Pinot Noir grapes were planted and flourished.

One maxim about living in wine country holds that "there is no forgetting that one is in wine country." Climb up the hillside through the oak forest and past the resevoir lake to see the views of Sonoma, Mount Tamalpais, and the Pacific Ocean unfold over

RIGHT: The terrace design integrates a deep floating overhang to provide protection from the elements. Four of Ron Mann's blue-gum eucalyptus chairs surround his Cloud steel table.

land and out to sea. The house sprawls into the views with a paved central courtyard that joins the main house to the guesthouse, a cabana, and the hillside wine cave.

The front entry is a few steps down from the drive and flows into the courtyard and a landing inlaid with redwood squares. The courtyard is also dressed with a blue-gum cypress bench that floats against a 90-degree angle along the exterior wall below the hammered-aluminum-and-steel light fixture by designer Ron

Mann. (The Sanchez's had long admired Mann's configurations and art-filled interiors.) The entrance is a floor-to-ceiling pivot door flanked by glass panels. The south terrace steps down to an open patio that features a steel-and-cast-concrete table and steel chairs with an olive tree and carved stone sculptures. Used for outdoor entertaining, the patio is separated from the spacious interior by glass walls. The interior is an open plan of living, dining, and kitchen areas, although there is no sense

OPPOSITE: In the great room, hand-tinted glazed-concrete floors and a hand-plastered ceiling form the backdrop for the floor-to-ceiling glass walls and a corten steel hearth. Ron Mann's sofas are blue-gum eucalyptus, sawed from single tree trunks. The cocktail tables are corten steel and sit on a cluster of dyed cowhide rugs.

RIGHT: In the gallery, which connects the guest house to the main house, the columns' placement and proportions create a beautiful play of natural light. At the end of the hall, two African Yoruba beaded headdresses sit atop custom-steel pedestals by Ron Mann.

BELOW: The glass wall along the western facade of the house opens the great room to the terrace that overlooks the sunset view.

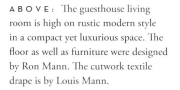ABOVE: The guesthouse living room is high on rustic modern style in a compact yet luxurious space. The floor as well as furniture were designed by Ron Mann. The cutwork textile drape is by Louis Mann.

RIGHT: The kitchen island combines three types of stone and steel with a cantilevered bay laurel countertop. The banana photomural is by Lenny Eiger. The perforated aluminum folding screens are by Ron Mann.

of the space being "one room." The entire space is surrounded by floor-to-ceiling glass walls and is anchored on the north side by a colonnade. The kitchen is inserted into the colonnade and defines the north wing of the house. The colonnade passes through the interior space and becomes a cantilevered viewing bridge over the outdoor pool in the back of the structure.

The back wall of the residence is composed of sliding-glass panels that permit the entirety of the interior to open to terraces and views. Local blue-gum eucalyptus trees were custom hewn to create large-scale sofas for the living area. The Ron Mann designs extend onto the terrace with individual seating around a low curved table. The wine caves were carved from the steep hillside on the 19-acre property and are flanked by natural rock formations. The interiors are walled with gunite, and there are three separate areas for entertaining, dining, and wine tasting, in addition to wine storage.

OPPOSITE: The wine cave was meant to be anything but traditional. Designed with cast-concrete walls and an arched gunnite ceiling, it has a lounge area and a dining area. Custom bay-laurel tables are surrounded by chairs from Wicker Wicker Wicker. The cocktail tables are by Ron Mann.

ABOVE: The master suite is an open floor plan with a flow from the sleeping area to the bath to the master dressing room. Ron Mann designed the headboard of the bed to asymmetrically project into the room and covered it with an Icelandic sheepskin blanket. Louise Mann's corner chairs are covered in her custom-print hemp textiles.

RIGHT: In a powder room in the main house, the dramatic cantilevered wood shelf with a case vessel sink is complemented by a corten framed mirror frame by Ron Mann.

PART III

Other Vines

"It was a spectacularly beautiful wine, and I still
have no idea if it was authentic," admitted
one wine expert who'd guzzled one of Kurniawan's
treasures. "It didn't really matter, to be honest."

—BIANCA BOSKER, *Cork Dork*

NARAMATA BENCH HOUSE

OWNERS: Anonymous

ARCHITECT: Sturgess Architecture

The Naramata Bench residence is perched on the edge of an ancient natural treasure of a lake called Okanagan Lake in British Columbia, Canada. There is nothing timid about it. The countryside around the lake is rugged, vivacious, scrappy, and strong. The lake itself is 84 miles long and very, very deep, reaching as far down as 761 feet at its deepest. It is wide enough to create distinct communities along the shoreline. The lake is between two to three miles wide in places as it curves its path along the way. The Naramata Bench is the site of a broad mantle of an ancient glacial drift on the lake's eastern edge. The "Bench" is a series of long, broad terraces—natural geological features that resemble steps moving down the sides of a valley as they were created by glacial ice and waters that receded in stages. The lake formed from overflow that ran along the sides of the moving, melting fields of ice. Flowing streams deposited residual minerals in the terraces of silt—primarily stone-free soil with distinct organic, matter-rich topsoils. Lake sediments form the white cliffs that are prominent and picturesque along the southern end of Okanagan Lake at the community of Penticton.

LEFT: The house is fronted by a young vineyard and features views out to the lake behind it.

The Naramata Bench is home to around two dozen wineries, each known for producing high-quality wine. When the Naramata Bench House project was initiated, Sturgess Architecture was brought on early in the process, prior to the final site selection. After surveying several potential sites in the area, the property on the bench definitely stood out. Due to its challenging and severe topography, the site was disregarded by the community and was identified as "unbuildable." Sturgess Architecture took the sublime location as a challenge, determined to embrace the unique natural, dramatic divergences of the site and to design a unique piece of architecture.

The 2.5-acre site, at the end of a cul-de-sac, reads as two parts. The upper half consists of an open, shallow slope, which is the new, still-maturing vineyard. The lower portion descends into a deep-forested gorge that carries the Naramata River to the south. Bridging the gap between the vineyard and the gorge, the long, narrow house is laid out in a linear pattern that links the two distinctive aspects of the site. The entire site overlooks the deep, fresh water of Okanagan Lake to the west.

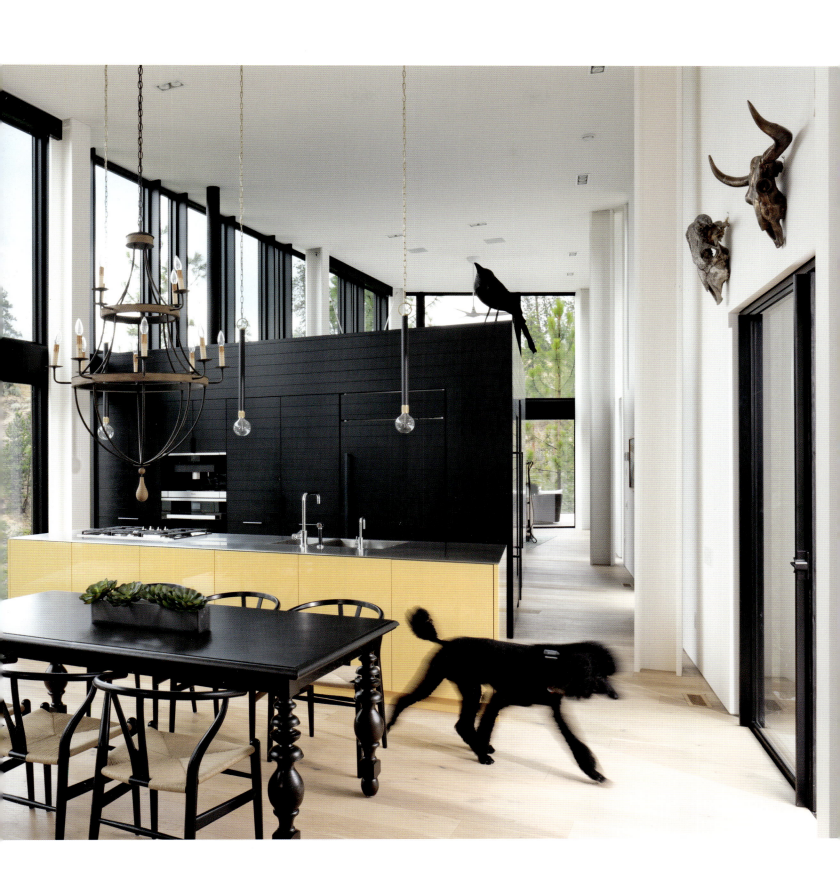

From the entrance drive, a concrete wall registers the privacy of the realm beyond, while a guesthouse suite overhangs the wall, offering a gesture of welcome. One approaches the house under the canopy of the guest suite to arrive at a framed view of the vineyard and the lake below. Entry is through a sequence of tall spaces that embrace both the wonder of the lake's blueness and the serene privacy of the vineyard. Inside, the enfilade of rooms narrows to ensure freedom from disturbances while the floor plan continues northward. The culmination is the main bedroom, with a highly dramatic cantilevered terrace above the gorge and the sounds of the rushing river below. The structure was built with

OPPOSITE: View west from the living room looking over the deep gorge toward Okanagan Lake.

ABOVE: The fireplace in the living room is surrounded by weathered-steel cladding.

this cantilever in mind in order to make room for the vineyard. At times, the owners claim, they feel as though they are living in the forest itself. The house faces west and catches the sun from morning until evening. At night, the lights from the small community of Summerland across the lake are worthy of toasting as they come alive after the sensational sunsets over the Okanagan.

OPPOSITE: The deck provides a spectacular sense of the wilderness of the surrounding valley and Okanagan Lake.

ABOVE: View to the master bedroom from a balcony cantilevered above the gorge.

LEFT: The embrace of the entry court serves to anchor the house to the landscape.

ABOVE: A louvered wall at the south terminal elevation of the house is a beautiful example of simplicity in form and material.

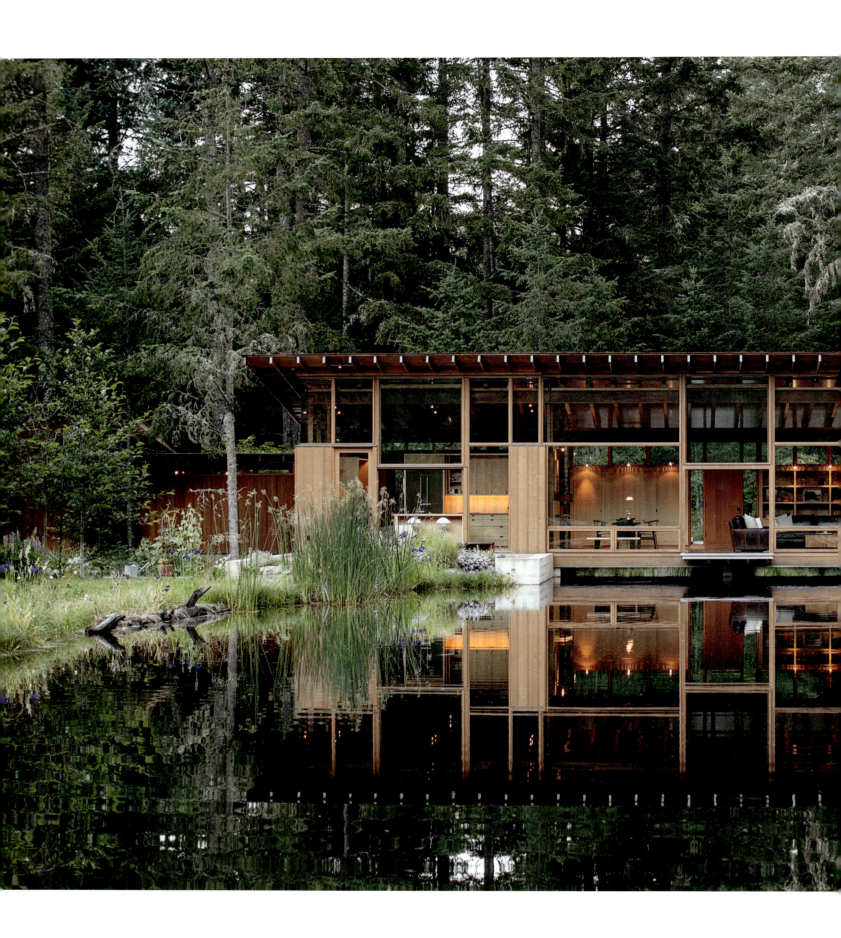

SEQUITUR VINEYARD

OWNERS: Michael Etzel and Carey Critchlow
ARCHITECT: James Cutler, Cutler Anderson Architects

The site is a 60-acre tree farm located in Oregon's premier grape-growing wine region. The land had been partially harvested by the previous owner, but much of the forest of oak, cedar, maple, and Douglas fir remained. Eighteen-plus acres were developed and planted as vineyard on a ridge above the house, up the hill from the residence, called Sequitur Vineyard. The vineyard is farmed organically and biodynamically and produces their delicious Pinot Noir.

When the architect walked the land with the new owners, they discovered an old, silted logging pond in an area of the land that was not conducive to cultivation. The architect felt that this would be a good site to entwine the lives of the family with the web of life that would surround them. The owners wanted "something remarkable, memorable, inviting, understated, and efficient." They wanted architecture that would connect humans and nature seamlessly as well as a dwelling that would provide warmth and protection from the natural world. The house features a zinc-and-cedar siding, which will weather naturally. The interiors are almost exclusively Douglas fir and cedar with red oak cabinetry. The three massive counter-weighted, vertical windows open for pure enjoyment of nature during contemplation and work.

LEFT: The southern facade of the house opens onto a picturesque pond.

The architect set the house on concrete piers that sit in the pond. A clear-spanned wooden shelter over the water uses steel columns and beams to minimize obstructions to the view while still allowing a warm wooden roof to shed the rain.

The owners live a very casual farming lifestyle, entertaining and hosting traveling wine lovers and wine writers, and have six children between them. They wanted a small-footprint house that would keep them connected to the land and their work in the vineyard but that would also offer quiet and peace. A small guesthouse can host overnight guests and is steps away from the main house. The separate unit can be "turned off and shut down" when not in use.

OPPOSITE: Through the open front door the pond reveals itself on the other side of the house.

ABOVE: The serenity of the site is the focus of the living and dining areas.

The house is in the center of an arboretum, where the life of the forest embraces daily living. The pond is as personal as any body of water can get. It offers constant movement: eagles, osprey (who love their rainbow trout), a blue heron named Herman, small green herons, cedar waxwings, wood ducks, crawfish, dragonflies, hawks, frogs, and more frogs, and honeybees. A large kitchen garden of vegetables and an herb garden flourish in the perfect maritime climate of the Ribbon Ridge AVA, just outside of Newberg, Oregon.

In the master bedroom, sleep is accompanied by the sounds of wildlife (which at times can be very loud), the touch of the forest air, the traces of the moon moving slowly across the sky, and perhaps a glimpse of Orion in the low eastern direction. Early morning before the sun rises over the ridge, is the freshest part of the day; and in evening, when the forest begins to come to life, the bats come out. And, oh, yes, there is a hammock at the far end of the pond for daydreaming.

ABOVE: The bedroom is encircled by a few newly planted trees and a lovely forest of Oregon fir.

OPPOSITE: In the autumn, the fireplace makes for cozy readying

TASTING ROOM, SOKOL BLOSSER WINERY & VINEYARDS

OWNERS: The Sokol Blosser Family
ARCHITECT: Brad Cloepfil, Allied Works Architecture

The Dundee Hills, the longtime home to the Sokol Blosser vineyards and winery, are recognized as one of the premier wine-growing appellations in the United States. The Dundee Hills AVA is a sub-appellation nested at the center of Oregon's Willamette Valley AVA. Willamette is the largest, and most popular, of Oregon's AVAs. It is a large section of the valley at 5,372 square miles, and modern Willamette Valley wine making began when a handful of bold and energetic young Californians began arriving there in the 1960s. They believed that Pinot Noir and, possibly, Chardonnay would flourish in that wet, rainy, foggy, unpredictable land. Susan Sokol Blosser and Bill Blosser were among the first to plant in the Dundee Hills in 1971. The hills, which were locally known as the Red Hills of Dundee, are rolling grasslands, oak trees, and Douglas firs. The winery buildings are spread across a knoll with 14 different vineyard blocks planted around the structures on the hillside, each block favoring its own rootstock and soil type.

LEFT: Sokol Blosser Winery has played a major role in creating Oregon's Yamhill County wine country, and their new tasting room is a welcome addition.

The site of the Sokol Blosser tasting room was planned as a series of terraces that follow the natural contours of the surrounding hills. The forms and expanse of the land are highlighted by the planting of the vines in parallel to disappear into the sun-touched rows, dipping into shady depressions and rising along hillsides into the late afternoon angles of greenness.

The design began by creating a series of gardens, terraces, and paths in the face of the hill. The new tasting room emerges as a solid mass of wood sliced open and carved out in response to natural light. It is reminiscent of a large fallen tree, heavy with bark and with a reddish color, and the terpenoid oils of

the interiors release the forest and marine fragrances that northwesterners live to inhale. The serene views and the rituals of wine tasting respond to the setting. It is a "transparent solid," a building that catches and holds space as light passes through. The angles of the interiors and framing of the building shift and bend as they foreshorten vistas and distort depths, intensifying the visitor's experience.

The elemental form and materiality draw inspiration from the earliest agricultural buildings in Oregon. Built of hemlock, fir, and cedar, these buildings had a close connection to the land and were constructed with economy and a sense of grace. The

LEFT: A striking feature of the exterior and interior of the tasting room is that surfaces are patterned with planks that are uneven, rough, and are not placed perpendicularly.

ABOVE: The building appears to be cut open from the outside, with skylights and lattices that allow patterned sunlight to move through the branches of a large tree.

FOLLOWING PAGES: The view of the vineyards from the front deck of the main building.

floors, walls, and ceiling of the interior are clad in rough-hewn cedar, the exterior a striated and random series of cedar boards. The faceted surfaces create a unified body of wood that holds the visitor to the hillside while connecting to the landscape beyond.

The building is organized to accommodate a range of wine-tasting experiences in distinct spaces: the main room, kitchen, library, cellar lounge, garden, porch, and terrace. A landscaped path guides visitors to the entry of the new tasting room; passing through the foyer and turning left, guests enter the main room. All interior surfaces are clad in cedar strips, creating a dynamic yet warm atmosphere suffused with light from both the expansive walls of glass on either side of the room as well as the narrow skylight that bisects the canted ceiling. The cellar lounge opens onto a garden, which is sheltered from general view by walls of board-formed concrete embedded in the earth and an overhanging grove of oak trees that anchor the western edge of the building. An exterior stair, which connects the main tasting room building to the outdoor terrace, leads from the front walk way to a grassy area behind the building and directly to the vineyards. Open to the elements on all four sides, the terrace provides sheltered views of the surrounding vineyards where Pinot Noir and Pinot Gris grapes are grown from numbered rootstocks and Jory soil.

OPPOSITE: Pure Oregon comfort: the more green one can see, the tastier the wine. View from the tasting room out to the porch and vista beyond.

ABOVE: At the entrance to the winery, visitors are welcomed by an intimate space for outdoor gatherings.

RIGHT: Spaces separate structures of the winery to allow the constant play of light among the cedar, fir, and hickory trees on the property.

CANOPY & GLASS HOUSE

OWNERS: Anonymous

ARCHITECT: David Coleman

A few miles east of Seattle is a wine-growing region called Woodinville, Washington, and its surrounds, which belong to the Puget Sound AVA. There are at least another 130 wineries in that AVA. (The mid-nineteenth-century migration of Italian and other European grape-growing immigrants landed in Washington state.) Life in the wine country of the Pacific Northwest is infused with the area's vibrant dynamism. It is a place where the zen of organic chemistry and the strength of character that farming requires has spread its influence.

The Canopy & Glass House was designed to become a part of a strong connectivity to its pastoral landscape. The clients longed for a house that was "full of light and close to nature." The desired goal was to provide comfort during Seattle's long, wet winters and to create an unabashed space for frolicking when summer and sun returned. To accomplish this, the owners and architect created a simple L-shaped plan for the house and pushed the building back toward a stand of cedar trees. This effort created a spacious front area where a powerful and quiet, meditative landscape would express composure, clarity, and tranquility.

LEFT: The house is built on terraces that move up the site, keeping the structure low and unified with its environment. Mature and majestic cedar groves enclose the permieter of the property and protect the house.

"Rooms"—some inside, some outside—were built to terrace up the hill and have interactions with one another. Entering through the driveway gate, one approaches through the tall trees into the auto court. This is the first of a series of outdoor rooms. The court is defined by concrete walls graced with vines. One then proceeds to an oversized stairway that leads to the meadow court, a spacious area planted in field grasses and with a sweeping Japanese maple, along with lots of blue sky and privacy in a corner dining area. Water flows between the stair and the house, softening the path and providing enough white noise to mask any sounds of a nearby road. The terrace court is the third outdoor room and is accessed from the living area. This is used for seasonal dining and evening campfires.

Inside, the house's rooms are organized into public and private wings. The roof over the public wing, supported by four concrete columns, is elemental, and pavilionlike, formed from a single sheet of material folded subtly in origami fashion to lighten its presence and push one's gaze out toward the landscape. Natural light flows freely inward. Inside and outside space are one visually; walls of glass define them functionally. The private wing houses family bedrooms and baths. Its low-slung roof and dark-colored finishes distinguish it visually from the public wing and suggest intimacy. A children's play loft is tucked under the great room roof, where the buildings intersect. A private terrace is located off the master bedroom.

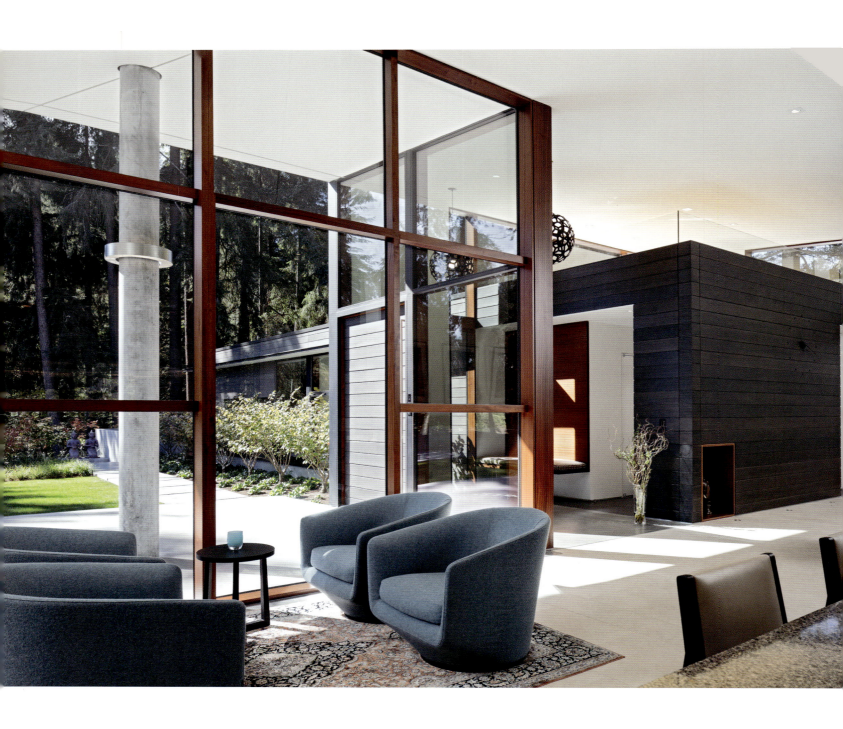

The material pallet is decidedly minimal, designed to reduce visual noise and strengthen the calming quality of the site: windows and doors provide warm wood frames for outward viewing; porcelain tile floors and concrete terraces create continuity between inside and out; white plaster walls and ceilings maintain brightness, even on gray days; blackened-steel hardware and trim provide contrast and visual interest. Sustainable features include geothermal heat, super insulation, passive solar with thermal mass, and wide overhangs for shade.

LEFT: The living room looks out onto the terrace court and is defined by a balance between daylight, privacy, and shelter. As part of the public spaces, the room flanks the darker-toned private wing containing the bedrooms. The roof over the public wing, supported by four concrete columns, creates an elemental pavilion seemingly formed from a single sheet of material.

ABOVE: Light fixtures and speakers are incorporated into the wood ceiling over the kitchen and dining areas.

ABOVE: The master bath is characterized by fluted wall tile and a wood-clad water closet designed as a piece of freestanding furniture.

RIGHT: The master suite is a refuge of comfort and tranquility. The built-in custom-upholstered window seat is a perfect spot for daydreaming.

NOVELTY HILL-
JANUIK WINERY

OWNERS: The Januik Family, Tom Alberg and Judi Beck
ARCHITECT: Mithun

This most enjoyable and perfectly stocked winery is deeply rooted in the famous school of Viticulture and Enology in 1880 at the California University, Davis. It is eye-opening to learn that the legislature California designated that the University of California would establish a program of research in viticulture and enology as part of a tremendous push for industry development. The experiment was interrupted by the enactment of Prohibition in the 1920. However, after the repeal of prohibition, the department regained its momentum in 1935, and the school has maintained its prestigious reputation as a source of master wine growers and producers.

Novelty Hill-Januik Wine is central to the wine country of the Seattle region. Novelty Hill Januik is a collaborative effort of two different wineries that operate from a spacious tasting room designed by Mithun architects. Mike Januik, a well-known master of the craft, makes the wine for both wineries. He was hired by

LEFT: The Novelty Hill-Januik Winery is spacious and welcoming. The architects intended that the structure would represent and reflect the Pacific Northwest at every turn.

LEFT: A red polycarbonate-panel fence against the shadows of adjacent evergreens.

OPPOSITE TOP: The interiors of Novelty Hill are perfectly suited for intimate tastings, large parties, and wonderful dinners.

OPPOSITE BOTTOM: The private cellar is meant for high cuisine and serious selections from winemaker Mike Januik's hand-crafted, world-appreciated Washington wines.

Tom Alberg and Judi Beck as a consultant for the planting of their estate vineyard, Stillwater Creek, located on the Royal Slope of the Frenchman Hills in Washington State's Columbia Valley, and he is one of the best-known wine makers in Washington. Virtually every grower would relish the opportunity to tap into his vast and thorough knowledge of the trade.

The western coastal states and British Columbia form a paradise of vineyards. Marine offshore air, fog and mist, rivers, glacial sediments, mountains, lakes, and inland deserts have all contributed to the thousands of unique types of terroir responsible for the fulsome flavors of grapes in each vineyard. Washington State is home to 940 wineries in 14 AVAs, with names like Ancient Lakes, Rattlesnake Hills, Columbia Gorge, and Walla Walla that are so descriptive it feels as though you are traveling through archaeological sites rather than lush and full-juiced fields of grapes.

WEATHERING SEATTLE HOUSE

OWNERS: Anonymous

ARCHITECT: E. Cobb Architects

The design of each interior space in this house was conceived so that all walls and doors open into or onto a rich exterior landscape or interior progression of experiences. A courtyard spans the entire northern length of the interior, flowing from the living area with sight lines into the interior and views of the lake through the dining space. Wind protection, water features, an outdoor fireplace, and luxurious greenery make the courtyard a place to enjoy day or evening. On the south side, with a welcome view of Lake Washington and of the all-encompassing Mount Rainier, the facade alternates as a series of pockets facing southwest, the ideal late afternoon exposure in Seattle.

The path of exterior spaces surrounding the house are mapped to the interior spaces for daily activities as well as panoramas of beautiful Lake Washington. The character of the landscape design is influenced by the mature natural landscape beyond. Farthest from the house, at the shoreline, the landscape is typical of a northwest forest, with evergreens, ground cover, ferns, and trails through the undergrowth. This landscape appears wild and fittingly adheres to a low degree of visible maintenance.

LEFT: In the back lawn, the site was excavated around a mature tree, with a concrete "planter" created to contain existing roots and soil mass.

OPPOSITE: Children's bedrooms occupy a corten-clad volume that cantilevers over a terrace, creating an outdoor living space.

FOLLOWING PAGES: The house features panoramic views of Lake Washington and Mount Rainier.

Winding paths and small structures create surprise encounters within the wilderness. Edging the top of the bank, the landscape features a flat recreational lawn and privacy hedges; existing mature trees are spaced deliberately, pruned and groomed to a mild perfection. The landscape adjacent to the house changes to become a "boxed landscape" of large and small containers.

The language of the house, in concrete, extends into the yard and takes various forms—blocks, planes, benches, and depressions—all of which contain plantings and natural materials. The compositions respond to views from the interior rooms and their seating arrangements. This enables a loose orthogonal set of reflecting pools on both the north and south sides of the house. Submerged planting boxes form islands in the pools, each containing specimen plantings. Retaining walls define the courtyard entry and hold large, descending planters with shore pines.

The zones of alternating interior and exterior spaces in this project are designed to convey a varied yet distinct character. This allows and, in many ways, encourages outdoor experiences at every turn. The variety and degree of sheltered alcoves and the detailed degree of planting engage one's sense of well-being in this remarkable collection of spaces.

TOP: View of the inner courtyard from the front door. Concrete planters, walkways, and benches appear to float above the water.

ABOVE: Rain creates reflections in the courtyard, with a blasting fire in the center, offering an unexpectedly lively visual experience for guests inside the living room.

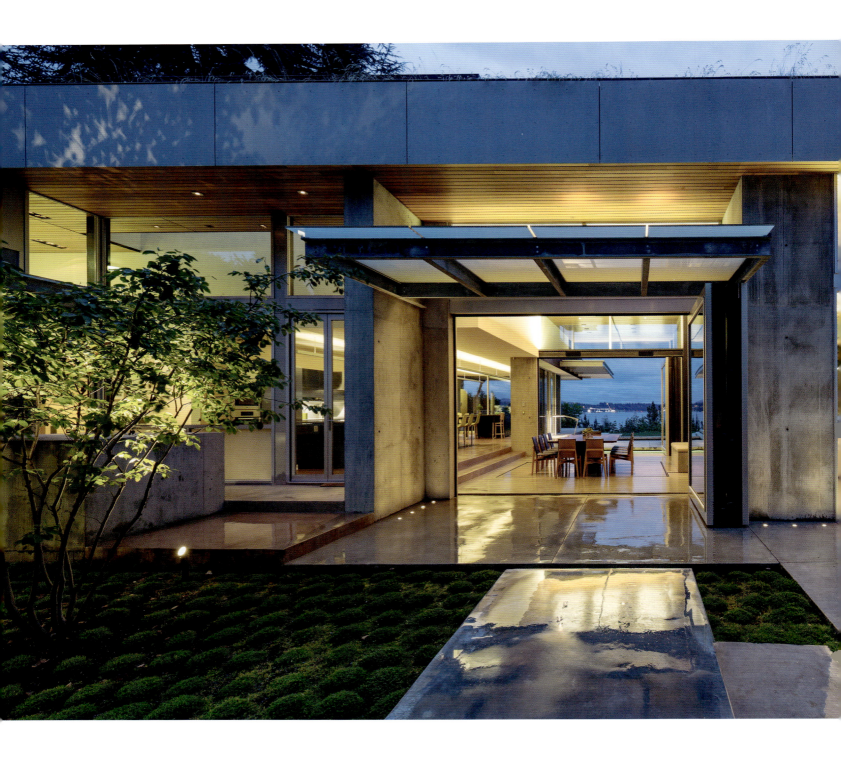

ABOVE: The view from the inner courtyard reveals the magic of the dining room, the rear terrace, the south lawn, and the evening lights on the opposite shore of Lake Washington.

OPPOSITE TOP: An inner courtyard off the guest suite features a tall chimney hovering over a concrete-base plinth surrounded by concrete seating. A mature blue Atlas cedar dominates the younger landscape of trees and vines.

OPPOSITE BOTTOM: View from the west side of the courtyard to the covered entry steps and ipe wood gate. Boston ivy and shore pine trees flank the steps.

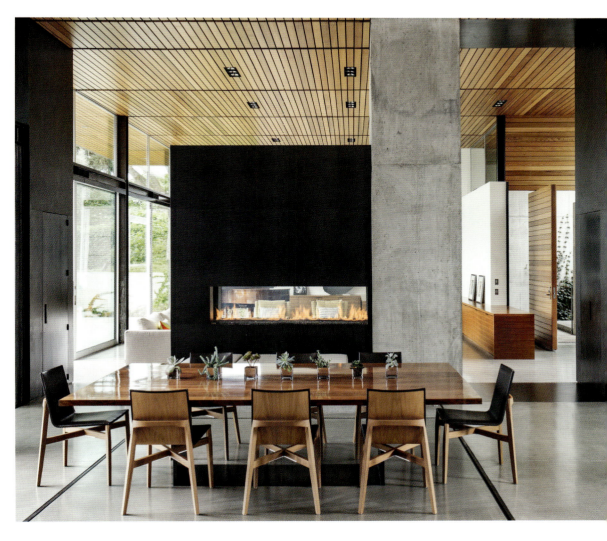

LEFT: The living room with the dining space and the kitchen beyond. The inner courtyard and guest suite are just outside the glass wall.

ABOVE: The dining room, on the opposite side of the fireplace from the living room. The fireplace is clad in blackened-steel plate. The 14-foot-high ceiling is detailed with cedar boards.

SOUTH OKANAGAN HOUSE

OWNERS: Anonymous

ARCHITECT: Allen + Maurer Architects

When this Vancouver couple decided, after eliminating a hefty list of options, to build their own summer home, they discovered this property above the scenic Naramata Bench, on Okanagan Lake, that had once been a part of a cherry and pear orchard. They selected a local architectural firm who, with an astute observation of the existing landscape, recommended removing the old, nonproducing fruit trees, resulting in an unobstructed 210-degree view of the lake and surrounding valleys. Their removal would also allow the design on the site to maximize exposure to the western light for the better part of the day.

The design scheme maintained a minimal footprint for the house, which virtually disappears into its setting. The clients' interests in fabric arts and photography required a large studio. The plan also required a large kitchen for entertaining. A central courtyard is flanked by a separate module on either side, requiring an outside passageway between the two. The open-air courtyard was treated as a part of the living area module, encircled in floor-to-ceiling glass, giving the entire house a much larger sense of space. The bedroom module is partly dug into the hillside and sports a green roof; both features offer added cooling to the house. The southern Okanagan region can get quite hot in the summer,

RIGHT: The house overlooks the legendary Okanagan Lake to the northwest. The glass pavilion contains the house's public living spaces, while the earth-sheltered structure to the right contains the bedrooms.

but the very hot weather lasts a relatively short time. Sliding walls in the living module allow the owners to take advantage of prevailing winds to cool the space. When needed, the house is heated by geothermal pumps.

The house is primarily used for the "bud break" through harvest season in the Okanagan. Favorite activities for the owners include early-morning bike rides and evening walks with their dog along a decommissioned rail line that runs along the edge of the mountain or along the lake a few minutes away down the hill. If the weather is inclement, the owners occupy their time with wine tastings at one of the 150 wineries on the Okanagan Bench, working on a project in the studio, or tending to their own small vineyard.

Bald eagles soar overhead, often as close as 10 meters above the house. California quail are especially entertaining when a parent is wrangling a brood of chicks through the vegetable garden. The sun is visible from the eastern end of the house along the southern edge until it sets behind the western mountains. The refractions of sunlight on the surface of the lake during the golden hour before sunset make this a favorite time. A significant population of deer is attracted by their love of grapes. Black bears are in the mountains along with cougar, elk (known here as wapiti), and the elusive bobcat. The skies are crowded with all varieties migrating of birds of the northwest regions including, of course, the ubiquitous Canada goose.

OPPOSITE: Past the glass pavilion and the corten-clad earth-shelter structure rests a sculptural gazebo resembling a sitting insect.

RIGHT: A formally planted courtyard separates the transparent living pavilion to the left from the earth-sheltered bedroom wing on the right.

BELOW: The glass pavilion emanates a glow at night. Architect-designed mounted light panels illuminate the surrounding terrace.

ABOVE: In the glass pavilion, the dining room offers views to the breathtaking lands of the Okanagan Valley.

LEFT: Pantry and other ancillary functions are placed in a "box" clad in "sundried tomato"–red panels, creating a dominant color scheme throughout the food preparation area and counter spaces.

RIGHT: The west facade of the glass pavilion is fully glazed, with mullions fastened to the steel structure. Sages and apple trees create a foreground to the panoramic view of Okanagan Lake.

MARTIN'S LANE WINERY

OWNER: Anthony von Mandl, VMF Estates
ARCHITECT: Tom Kundig, Olson Kundig Architects

There are many characteristics of Tom Kundig's architecture that make everything he designs affect humans on an emotional plane. One of those is a belief that buildings should be subordinate to the larger landscape. In other words, "the wine should never overwhelm the trout." Martin's Lane Winery embodies this maxim. It is difficult to decide which should receive your attention first—the architecture or its surrounding landscape. The topography of the site entwines itself around the structure until at last the building appears as if it is floating in a crush of grapevines.

Martin's Lane has its own integrated purpose. It was dug out of the steep side of a small mountain. The winery is a six-step production center and is built on the hillside to utilize the downward slope for a gravity-flow wine-making process. The six stepped levels of this process are designed to make wines with the very least mechanical intervention. The other side of the building comprises a visitor center, offices, and a private tasting room that cantilevers over the vineyards and offers sweeping views of nearby Okanagan Lake.

RIGHT: The vineyards of Martin's Lane Winery rise above nearby Okanagan Lake and provide visitors with spectacular views.

The grape-receiving area at Martin's Lane is at the top of the slope, then comes the fermentation and the settling room, down to the bottling room above ground level; the barrel storage area is below ground. Throughout the winery's 34,800 square feet, the office, wine lab, and visitor spaces are woven into the manufacturing areas, including tasting room, dining room, and visitor walkways that offer intimate glimpses of the production process. The design's central "fracture" allows for an expansive line of clerestory windows that increase natural daylight intake into the production areas as well as open impressive views of the surrounding vineyards

RIGHT: Architect Tom Kundig's design for the winery is expressive of the power and mystery of the land, sea, and skies of the Okanagan Valley.

BELOW: The winery building is a symphony of tilted planes that reflect the dramatically sloping site.

LEFT: Spectacular clerestory windows extend the entire length of the main structure.

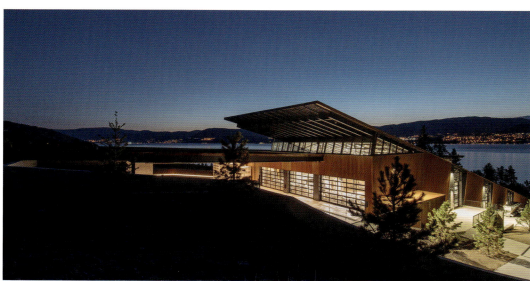

and natural landscape. The building's exterior is clad with obsidian-painted structural steel, while rusted corrugated steel is used for siding and roof overhangs. Siding panels are tilted downhill to visually underscore the story of the gravity-flow process.

Visitors enter the facility through a rough-formed concrete tunnel to a private tasting room accented by a glass-and-perforated-steel wall that overlooks the barrel storage area. A custom-designed-and-fabricated spiral-steel staircase leads up to a larger tasting room and visitor experience. The form of the staircase was inspired by the stainless steel filtering equipment used in the wine industry as well as by the Fibonacci sequence, which is used to show how grapevines propagate.

LEFT: A tasting room offers stunning views of Okanagan Lake, with the custom-designed, amorphous table reflecting the lake's form.

RIGHT: The winery's Barrel Room is distinguished by its evocative lighting scheme.

BELOW RIGHT: The form of the staircase was inspired by the gravity-flow technique used in winemaking, a means of less harsh mechanical production.

RED MOUNTAIN
VINEYARD RESIDENCE

OWNERS: Robert V. Taylor and Jerry D. Smith
ARCHITECT: Tom Kundig, Olson Kundig Architects

Growing conditions are supremely different in Washington State than in any other wine growing region in the West. The number one difference is that the vineyards are several hours inland from the Pacific coast. The Red Mountain AVA gets its name from the short, red, fruiting plant called *Bromus japonicus.* It is the jewel red of a young merlot with slightly orange tones. The AVAs that surround Red Mountain are the Horse Heaven Hills AVA, the larger Columbia Valley AVA, and the Yakima AVA, which was the first AVA to be established in Washington State, in 1983. Each appellation has its own distinctive microclimate affecting the terroir. For example, the soil in the Red Mountain AVA is very gravelly and highly alkaline. A mantle of dunes that vary in thickness encircling Red Mountain has created a series of soils that differ from those of the other surrounding AVAs. Also, the vineyards in eastern Washington are in the rain shadow of the Cascade Range, where irrigation is essential and water rights are tightly controlled.

RIGHT: The beauty of the house is amplified by its seclusion within the surrounding vineyards, particularly at dusk.

Owners Robert V. Taylor and Jerry D. Smith decided to build their seasonal home in Benton County on a site that was originally chosen in the 1980s by Smith's father, who founded a grapevine nursery business nearby. Smith knew the potential of the location, having lived there as a child, and the quietude and privacy of it particularly appealed to him. Smith and Taylor live in a house designed by Tom Kundig and built in the midst of their vineyards and orchards. A new swimming pool is currently under construction adjacent to the outdoor patio and fireplace. The primary materials used in the construction are steel, glass, aluminum, and concrete.

Smith and Taylor grow and provide the purest rootstock from their 150-acre nursery and have developed their products here for over 40 years. Over those years, they have worked with the local growers to manage the long-term sustainable development of their vineyards.

ABOVE: This region of Washington State is reported to have 300 days of sunshine a year, with only seven inches of rain. And yet the house is surrounded by vineyards on the south side and a blueberry farm on the north side.

RIGHT: View of the house toward the Horse Heaven Hills to the south. Outdoor seating and dining areas allow large parties or small groups to gather around the fireplace.

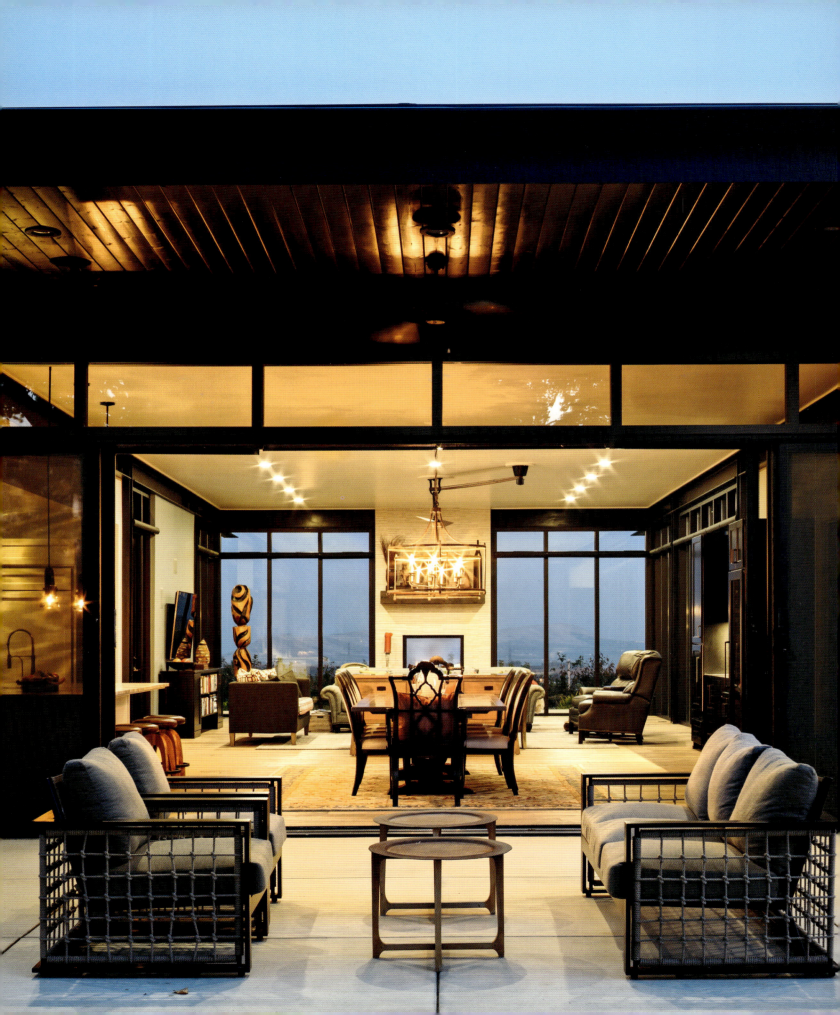

OPPOSITE: Entertainment and living areas open to the outdoor terraces through large sliding glass walls.

ABOVE: In the backyard, a mature maple tree provides shade for the abundant seating area.

LEFT: The living room has glass walls on all sides, which offer panoramic views of the surrounding vineyards. Automatic panels can be lowered to shade the south facing glazing from extreme sun and heat.

TOP: Kitchen has sufficient space for several cooks to be prepare dishes simultaneously as well as an enclosed pantry and a full dining area close for serving.

ABOVE: View from the master bedroom to the master bath, full dressing area, closet, and large vanity. The soaking tub fills from a full cascading shower in the ceiling.

SANTA LUCIA PRESERVE

OWNERS: Anonymous

ARCHITECT: Sagan Piechota Architecture

There is a Carmel Valley AVA, although this and other smaller grape-growing regions may be overshadowed by the legendary vineyards to the north. After all, West Coast vineyards from Santa Barbara to British Columbia do share, if never their terroir, their stories, which are always a variation on the theme of the brave and bold French, German, Spanish, Italian, Hispanic, monastic, and other immigrants who carried seeds or plants to this coastal region and found their planting paradise. The story of Monterey County wine stretches back more than two centuries to some of the earliest days of wine in California. The French missionaries who settled in the Monterey area during the late 1700s not only grew grapes for sacramental wine but occasionally to drink for pleasure. They also served their homemade wines—generally made of muscat and mission grapes—to guests and travelers. Today, more than 250 years later, wine maintains its vital position and importance in the powerful California soils.

LEFT: The approach to and entry facade of the house both feature landscape design by Bernard Trainor + Associates.

Blessed with a long growing season and temperate climate, the Monterey AVA now produces the most Pinot Noir in all of California and sustains the number two spot for Chardonnay production. The Monterey AVA stretches 100 miles, from the tip of Monterey Bay to the border of Paso Robles in the south. Offshore winds from the coast flow through swaths of the Salinas and Carmel valleys. The valleys are abundant in sandy and gravelly loam soils, which are nutrient poor and free draining, causing vines to struggle to grow deep root systems to reach water in the ground. It is believed that this struggle increases grape's flavor complexity. Monterey is also home to five sub-AVAs, including the Carmel Valley, Santa Lucia Highlands, and Arroyo Seco, which reflect the area's diversity of mesoclimates (the climate of a particular vineyard) and microclimates (that of a row of vines).

Daniel Piechota designed a house on an eight-acre parcel in Carmel's Santa Lucia Preserve, which sits in the center of the Carmel Valley AVA, a small grape-growing region within the Monterey AVA. This is precious wine country, and the property sits within 10 miles of the nearest vineyards and so is part of a conservation plan. The soft and sensual hills, the robust and rugged oak trees, the small family herds of deer that frequently appear all drew the owners to purchase the property. The design of the house would respect and respond to the qualities of a composed and gentle way of living.

LEFT: View at dusk across the house's central courtyard to the living room.

BELOW: The covered terrace adjacent to the living room features an outdoor fireplace.

Walking the property to discover is best features is the most accurate way to learn everything an architect might use in the design process: the angles of the sun, positions of the moon, where Orion comes up in the east, animal trails, migrations patterns in the sky and on land, which ways the wind will blow, where the streams flow and what lives in them. I have known architects who have camped out on-site to capture the exact movements of stars for skylights. For an architect, walking the property dozens of times will instill a natural plan in his or her mind for the design and help when an owner wants to know what he or she will be looking at while dressing in the morning. Here, Piechota positioned the living area so that it overlooks an adjacent oak grove, giving a lovely sensation of living in a tree house. The house is designed so that all views, both large and small, can be appreciated by the viewer. For example, some views can be seen from only from a particular window in the structure, such as a very narrow

one in the opening of a wall that frames a single old-growth oak. Piechota has also created floor-to-ceiling windows for panoramic views into the valley. From the exterior, the curve of the drive up to the large horizontal volumes, the angles of the negative spaces, and the broad steps express a slowing down, a calming among the well-being of the oaks. As you approach the house, you begin to experience the zen of the place. The totality of the house is an expression of pleasure, composure, the world as it should be.

ABOVE LEFT: View from the covered terrace with fireplace to the central courtyard.

TOP: The covered terrace leads out and up a gentle slope to a welcoming firepit in the distance.

ABOVE: Across the central courtyard, another covered terrace features an outdoor hot tub, situated between the master bedroom and the guest house.

LEFT: The front entrance to the house, where the decks are built around the existing beautiful old live oaks.

BELOW: View from the central courtyard down the entry stairs.

OPPOSITE: The front facade of the house features metal-clad garage doors.

OPPOSITE: View from the outdoor fireplace terrace to the valley below, populated by wild native deer and rolling hills.

LEFT: A glass-enclosed bridge extends over the exterior entry stair sequence outside.

BELOW: The northeastern corner of the living room offers panoramic views of the valley landscape for miles.

PART IV

Napa

Although "unicorn wines" share the same highly
fetishized aura that surrounds the kind of blue-chip
trophy wines collectors have always vied for...they
confer status not by virtue of their cost, which varies,
but the special expertise it takes to acquire them.

—ZACHERY SUSSMAN,
"Unicorn Wines," *The World of Fine Wine*

SENTINEL RIDGE
VINEYARD RESIDENCE

OWNERS: Anonymous

ARCHITECT: Jess Field, Field Architecture

Sentinel Ridge stretches across the brow of a winding grade break on Howell Mountain, which overlooks all of Napa Valley. The dramatic mountain site high above the valley is a wilderness that in itself requires a commitment to reach. The site is extraordinary, and an accurate reading of it was critical. Rigorous studies of the geology, hydrology, and solar and wind patterns were undertaken, as well as of the wildlife migration patterns. The nuances and characteristics of the land would drive the design rather than encumber it. For example, rather than blast the hard rock surfaces to create a deep foundation, the architects determined that anchoring the structures directly to the rock would result in the most advantageous way to unify the construction site, which lies between the cultivated vineyards on one side and native forest on the other. The resulting design of the residence reveals the most spectacular as well as intimate characteristics of the site's topography, climatological influences, and tree growth—its combined terroir.

RIGHT: Situated at the edge of the vineyard and along the precipice of the forest beyond, Sentinel Ridge demonstrates the unification of how the two landscapes create a powerful sense of place.

The project is composed of three buildings situated on a single concrete base that reflects the natural steps and terraces of the land composed of an aggregate mixed with site rock, the smooth troweled tops and the vertical board-formed sides of the structures generate the sense that the base itself is being "upheaved" from the rocks below.

The material language is raw and natural. Both the interiors and exteriors of the buildings use reclaimed old-growth Douglas fir in hues reflecting the densities and lightness of the forest— deep browns, reds, and silvers—in combination with steel, concrete, and glass. The buildings resonate with the cultural heritage and simplicity of the region's vernacular while powerfully suggesting in its materials and their assembly forward movement into the twenty-first century.

The interiors are simple and comfortable. Interior designer Erin Martin maintained a monastic and spacious minimalism. The open living area in the center of the design is a haven for small or large gatherings, which can be managed with built-in design elements such as a large table on iron tracks that can take center stage or be moved off to the side for tasting parties. Private spaces all share a luxurious collection of angles, light, and serene colors. Functional wood sculptures are put to use as small tables, a headboard, and accessories. Rooms in the sleeping wing all open to a small outdoor terrace facing either the vineyards or the forest. Martin is right to claim that when there is so much beauty just outside surrounding every interior space, one doesn't need much more than what is already there naturally.

OPPOSITE: The central barn space, with its large wooden pivot doors, is flanked on either side by two wings with colonnades.

RIGHT: The house is conceived as three gabled volumes linked together with an outdoor colonnade that threads through the buildings and functions as the main circulation spine.

BELOW: The house's design draws on agrarian forms to create a highly functional and contemporary building.

PREVIOUS PAGES: Large sliding doors open on both sides of the barn, opening a grand dining space the lavish vineyard on one side and fresh-scented pines on the other.

ABOVE: The house is designed using a minimal palette of blackened steel, reclaimed wood, concrete, and plaster all expressed in unique combinations in each of the spaces.

RIGHT: Large plaster walls capture sunlight through a dormer, whose form is expressed through meticulously detailed timber-and-steel trusses. The dining table is built on a steel carriage frame and slides along tracks cast into the concrete floor to function as a wine-tasting table. The pendant light fixture is repurposed from a steel ocean buoy.

LEFT: In the kitchen, a partial wall of bright-white cabinetry offers a striking contrast to the reclaimed wood of the ceilings and walls.

RIGHT: The headboard in the master bedroom is composed of a bronzed mirror set into a sliding steel frame. Reflections of the forest beyond create the sensation of the bed floating in the trees.

BELOW: Each of the guest rooms has a unique view and private access to the forested landscape.

RUTHERFORD VINEYARD RESIDENCE

OWNERS: Anonymous

ARCHITECT: Johnson Fain Architects

This residence is built upon a hillside at the top of a 42-acre site that looks out over its vineyards to the southwest and the valley below. The house was designed as a country home and office for clients who enjoy entertaining. One approaches the entry to the house through a field of tufa stone, while the back portion of the house, with its views through the glass walls of the living area, faces into a grove of scrub oak and native plants. In addition to the property, four acres of hillside have been planted in volcanic soil to cultivate Cabernet Sauvignon.

The house emerges from its wooded, flat portion of the hilltop site as a contrast to the landscape while also expressing a natural integration into the landscape. The house is a modern and ordered series of rectilinear volumes clad in precise and beautifully finished, dark corrugated-steel siding materials. With the house an integral part of the landscape, components such as the central living space with its floor-to-ceiling glass walls and glass clerestory to the roof edge do nothing to interfere with the uniquely framed views of the clusters of oaks and the landscape beyond. The floor plan was carefully arranged to preserve as many

of the tufa boulders and oak trees that surround the house as possible. The 75-foot lap pool at the rear of the house draws one's gaze into the rear grove. Slender support columns carry a cantilevered roof of exposed-wood beams out over a barbecue area with an exterior fireplace; the beams also subtly hint at the surrounding trees and moss-covered stones that filter sunlight down the edges of the pool.

On a cloudy day—with breezes blowing the tall grasses that lead to front of the glass entry, the trees showing through

the glass, and reflections of the skies and clouds—the slender horizontal line of the roof is scarcely visible. The house virtually disappears into the gathering reflective chaos. Interior finishes include glass-mosaic-tiled bathroom floors and walls, suspended ceilings, ebonized-and-stained-maple-veneer millwork, and silver travertine accents and brushed stainless steel hardware. Polished concrete floors throughout meet the rich texture of cleft quartzite-stone stairs. Textiles for furnishing draw inspiration from the property's lovely hues of lichens, slates, and mosses.

ABOVE: At the house's entrance, large limestone pavers are placed amid mounds of native grasses.

FOLLOWING PAGES: The limestone-lined, infinity-edged pool is surrounded by oak trees.

OPPOSITE: Limestone pavers and native grasses foreground the view through to the living room to the patio and pool.

ABOVE: The pool offers views through the surrounding oaks to the bucolic valley below.

RIGHT: The living room and dining area occupy the center of the house.

LEFT: View of the dining area to the breakfast nook and kitchen.

RIGHT: The guest bedroom opens to the forested backyard.

BELOW: Open-beamed ceilings extend throughout the house, including the master bedroom.

JAMES COLE
ESTATE WINERY

OWNERS: Colleen Harder and James Harder
ARCHITECT: John David Rulon

The Napa Valley isn't nearly as large as its reputation would suggest. Defined by the Vaca Mountains to the east and the Mayacamas Mountains to the west, Napa is one of the smallest wine-growing regions in the world. Thirty miles of valley are divided by a winding river, and the lowest parts of the valley are five miles wide. A critical range of temperatures depends on the ocean fog, which moderates those temperatures to maintain a desired balance in the grapes between the sugars and the acids.

The Napa Valley is a unique wine-growing region with a complex tapestry of vineyard locations that possess individual personalities through soil and climate. The hills that cover the terrain above and around the valley floor were created by ancient landslides in the Vaca Mountains centuries ago. They carved dips, caves, and recessed hills and pushed vast regions of soils that became the knolls of the valley. Each vineyard, however small, is subject to its own specific climate patterns.

LEFT: James Cole Cabernet Sauvignon vineyard rows with winery the background. Entrance to the winery is just below the dormer window.

TOP: The front patio of the winery serves as a private tasting area as well as a seasonal entrance to the winery's interior tasting room.

ABOVE: Verbena, salvia, and rose bushes flank the gravel promenade and the large-scale outdoor chess set in the winery garden between the tasting room and bocce court.

ABOVE RIGHT: Garden gazebo next to bocce court.

James and Colleen Harder purchased this 11-acre property—then a dilapidated equestrian center—in 2000, and they planted the vineyard soon after their purchase. The winery building sits on the footprint of one of the original buildings. Nine of the eleven acres are planted with three clones of Cabernet Sauvignon. Fruit from each clone is kept separate during the aging process and then blended for the final wine. All production is very limited, with each wine in the 100- to 400-case range and total production around 750 cases. The first vintage of James Cole Estate was 2003. The winery specializes in Cabernet Sauvignon, which makes sense based on their location just south of the famous Stags Leap District AVA, one of the best-known Cabernet Sauvignon–producing districts in Napa Valley.

The vineyards surround the stone building that houses the fermentation tank room, barrel room, tasting room, and kitchen. A small second-floor office loft overlooks the tasting room with views both through the winery and out a large window facing the front vineyards and the Silverado Trail, which is a short distance away.

OPPOSITE: The chandelier in the tasting room was made from a twenty-year-old cracked and weathered oak branch from the Rijsterbos forest in the Netherlands.

ABOVE: The barrel room features a handmade table derived from steamed barrel staves and vineyard endposts. Classic movies often play on the drop-down screen, and vintage motorcycles are displayed along the room's perimeter.

ZINFANDEL VINEYARDS RESIDENCE

OWNERS: Anonymous
ARCHITECT: Field Architecture

Built on one of the oldest cultivated Zinfandel vineyards on the valley floor, this house was sited alongside a stand of 300-year-old oak trees that form a windbreak for the 20-acre property, echoing their form in the three wings through which the residence stretches into the landscape. On one end, a majestic valley oak forms a peak in the long valley; this landmark participates in the conversation with the two long mountains of Sugarloaf Ridge that shield the eastern horizon. The project orients itself toward these two landmarks with an organizational axis, off which the forms of the new farmhouse can shift and slide. The essence of the area was distilled—complete with working vineyards, ancient trees, and long-standing structures—into a series of forms that adjust and respond to the existing conditions. With the vineyard conceptualized as ground and the mountains and tree as figure, they became anchors for the main axis of the project, allowing the house to knit itself into the land.

RIGHT: A simple palette of materials and meticulous detailing elevate the overall design of the house, seen here from the vineyard at dusk.

The core of the design program developed from the need to accommodate both small and large gatherings, infusing it with a playful balance of connection and privacy that could bring everyone closer to the land and to one another. The gathering spaces are centrally located and face inward, while the private spaces are pulled out to the periphery, facing the long shelter of the valley. Central to the project was the challenge of creating a contemporary expression of the age-old typology of the farmhouse while pushing the envelope of contemporary construction. An old barn on the property was repurposed to house an intimate gathering space that pulls one through the vineyard toward the mountains to the west, tying the residence to both its own long history and the ancient forms of its larger landscape. The house demonstrates how basic vernacular strategies can be leveraged as contemporary formal devices to knit the building into the landscape. A clear material expression was enabled by rich wood that punctuates a sleek, airy, modern interior, the deep contrast offering both textural structure and visual rhythm. And the overall compound is organized to produce a wind-sheltered courtyard within the larger embrace of a stand of oaks: a layer of building within a layer of landscape.

OPPOSITE: The pool house opens onto a reclaimed-teak deck.

ABOVE: Arrival to the house is signaled by the carport, with steel windows framing the open end of the gable.

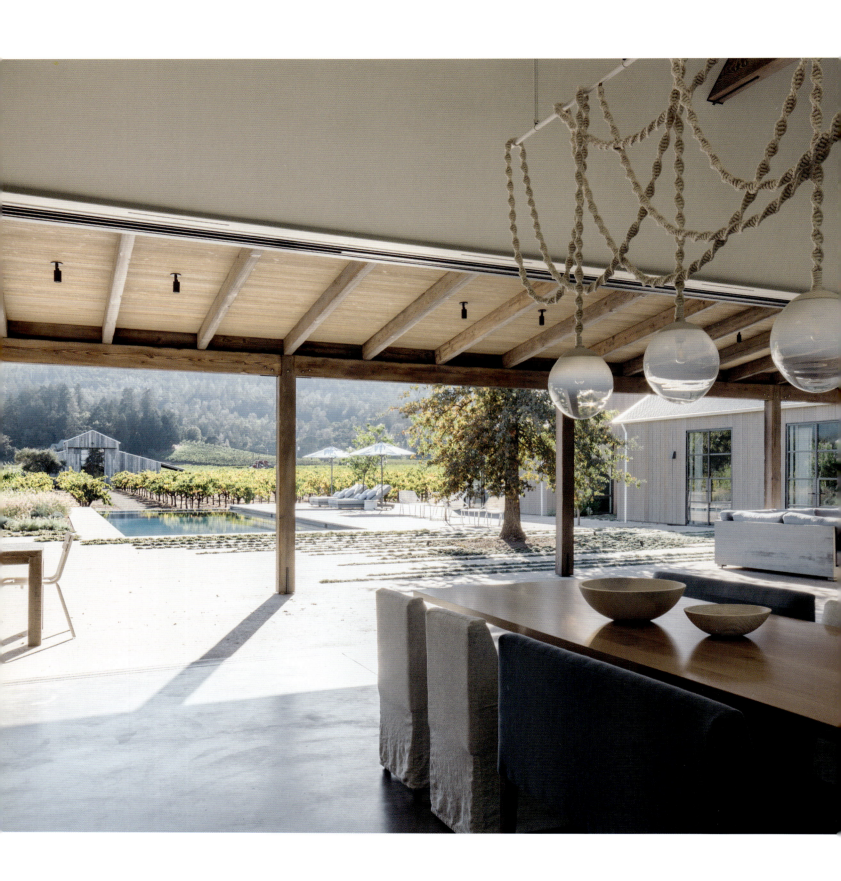

LEFT: When open, an expanse of sliding glass panels extends the living room out to the courtyard and invites views to the pool and barn beyond.

ABOVE: Oak cabinetry is combined with concrete countertops to create the material palette for the kitchen.

ABOVE LEFT: Timber trusses frame the master bedroom.

LEFT: In a guest room, bunk beds are fabricated of blackened steel.

ABOVE: Rich wood trusses punctuate the airy, modern interior, which is bookended by tall cement-like plaster walls.

OPPOSITE: The barn features a mezzanine, exposed timber trusses, and a metal-and-blown-glass chandelier by Longhouse.

MACAYAMAS MOUNTAIN RESIDENCE

OWNERS: Richard and Tatwina Lee
ARCHITECT: Steven Harris Architects

Elliot Lee, a partner at Steven Harris Architects, designed this house as a weekend retreat for his parents. It was one of the first projects to go through the Napa Valley Viewshed Ordinance, which governs and conserves the steep hillsides and scenic ridges that appear throughout the Napa Valley. Lee's house tested the new criteria, which has since become standard. The house is a minimal insertion into a narrow ridge, and it spreads along the site to take full advantage of the shifting views of the valley throughout the day. The house is surrounded by alfresco dining space, garden terraces, a swimming pool, and a vegetable garden.

The site has a unique history: the entire area was denuded of its native redwood trees to rebuild San Francisco after the 1906 earthquake. Before that, it had been virgin land, covered with native plants and one mere footpath that had been cleared by a lone backhoe. Later, in the 1950s, it was seeded with non-native

LEFT: The living room, seen here at dusk, opens onto its own private terrace and overlooks stand of olive trees framing the view of Diamond Mountain.

pines from airplanes after a fire up-valley. After that, many fallen and dying pines made for treacherous surveying of the ridge. All along and below the ridge was Napa Valley and Mt. Saint Helena on the eastern side, while on the western side one could see into the vineyards of the Diamond Mountain AVA. The house sits lightly on the site and has become one with the natural landscape of the ridge, capturing the spirit the surrounding vineyards, valleys, and mountains.

The interiors of the house give the feeling that the outside is only a step away, as if life is always lived out on the ridge.

The owners are most happy in the large living area of the main house where they can observe both valleys at once and enjoy the occasional bobcat or fox walking in front the windows. Both Tatwina's and Richard's families immigrated to the area from Pearl River Delta four generations ago, and members of their families may have even worked to build the first wineries in the valley. Whatever the case, they had long been drawn to have a relationship with this land and now even grow vegetable and fruit heirlooms, Western and Asian, and, yes, they do have a few grapevines in their garden.

OPPOSITE: The main house is sited in the saddle of a ridgeline in order to blend into the topography of the site.

RIGHT: The lap pool extends from the rammed-earth wall of the main house to end at the pool terrace.

BELOW: The pool terrace offers beautifully framed views northeast to Mount Saint Helena.

LEFT: The graveled, semi-enclosed outdoor dining area features a trellis made of weathering steel, rammed-earth walls, and lush landscaping.

TOP: The entry path to the dining area winds down from the top of the ridge to the outdoor dining area.

ABOVE: The outdoor dining room is protected by rammed-earth walls on three sides and, on the fourth side, by original rock formations on the ridge.

ABOVE: A window seat in the living room overlooks old oak trees that were protected during the construction of the house.

RIGHT: The doors along the rammed-earth wall slide completely out of view, effectively turning the kitchen and living areas into covered outdoor rooms. The walls are complemented by a cedar ceiling, bubinga wood cabinets, bamboo-and-cast-stone countertops, and concrete floors seeded with stone harvested from the property.

OPPOSITE: The master suite is located at the secluded north end of the ridge, a short walk from the main building.

ABOVE: The corner window has a screened view to the west of the vineyards at the top of Diamond Montain and a view to the north of the indigenous madrones and manzanitas. The steel-and-glass window system was designed to support the built-in walnut desk.

OAK KNOLL VINEYARD RESIDENCE

OWNERS: Anonymous
ARCHITECT: Swatt Miers Architects

The site of this house had been on the owners' radar for many years, having long admired it as they passed by on bicycle rides through the Napa Valley. It is 4.5 acres of Cabernet Sauvignon vineyards on an oak-studded knoll. The dream started to become a reality when the property became available and the clients embarked on their journey to create their wine country dream home. Several magnificent old oak trees surround the site and there are daydream views in almost every direction. The owners wished to preserve the heritage oaks that dot the knoll, to allow for views of the sunsets over the Silverado Trail to the west, and to have generous family and outdoor living and entertaining areas oriented to the quiet, east side of the property that faced the endless row of vineyards and the rolling hills.

RIGHT: The house maintains a striking modern profile among the surrounding vineyards and oak trees.

The owners carried out an exhaustive search for a compatible architectural firm to partner with to design their home. They chose Swatt Miers to bring their ideas to life. To make certain that would happen, very early on in the relationship the owners presented Robert Swatt with a 50-page document outlining everything they wanted for their home, room by room, view by view, season to season, sunrise to sunset. There had to be harmony between the structure and the land, with all human-made contributions being rectilinear and nature balancing the house with the curvatures of the surrounding landscape. Due to the owner's passion for technology and living "green," the house is run mostly off solar energy. Natural materials used in the house include honed native Mount Saint Helena tufa limestone, quarried in the late 1800s to early 1900s, and swaths of sustainable wood that beautifully finish the interior and the exterior.

The lady of the house, if asked, would narrow her favorite room to either the master suite or the great room that is comprised of the kitchen, dining area, and living space and leads out to the pool. The master suite, however, is her sanctuary, reached only by a glass-and-steel bridge. Its minimalist atmosphere creates a sense of

ABOVE: At dusk, the stair tower adjacent to the entry glows like a lantern.

RIGHT: The master bedroom deck cantilevers into the oak trees. All of the heritage oak trees on the property were preserved.

FOLLOWING PAGES: The pool at the east side of the house overlooks the mountain landscape.

calm and privacy in an otherwise open living environment. Half of the master bedroom is glassed-in with floor-to-ceiling walls and sliding doors. The outdoor deck juts into the trees, which come alive with sights and sounds of turtledoves and other birds.

The gentleman of the house, when pressed, may choose the acoustically mastered music/media room, which was designed over a four-year period. The owners and the architects share a deep and genuine love for music, and the room's equipment was chosen to combine the best of the latest digital and classic analog audio and visual equipment to provide the richest possible listening and viewing experiences, and the decor serves to highlight albums that in their own way provide the soundtrack to the owner's life.

OPPOSITE: The kitchen looks west to oak trees and vineyards beyond.

ABOVE: View from the great room to the pool entrance and vineyards.

RIGHT: Stairway down to the wine cellar.

OPPOSITE AND TOP:
Sliding floor-to-ceiling glass panels
open the galley kitchen to the
property's southwest vineyards. The
kitchen counter with bar on the
dining room side.

ABOVE: The master bath features
a view through a stand of oaks to the
vineyard.

OAK KNOLL DISTRICT RESIDENCE

OWNERS: Anonymous

ARCHITECTS: Brandon Jørgensen, Atelier Jørgensen

The owners of this house wanted foremost to display their large art collection and to entertain their friends and family. They both also wanted a gardens and cozy places that were separate from their guests. Architect Brandon Jørgensen executed that vision beautifully by creating two separate structures. The owners love being connected to their gardens, and they love watching the sunset over the hills while sitting on the spacious terrace.

The site comprises a large piece of land dotted with full-grown trees and set within the vineyards and two houses connected with glass. Each house is protected from a busy road with two L-shaped walls, one of stone and one of cedar. The entire house occupies a single level, giving it a low profile close to the earth. A sequence of individual gardens is designed so that each maintains its own unique complexion and flavor. The house's courtyards, gardens, and interior spaces all embrace and respect the surrounding natural landscape.

RIGHT: The material pallette of architect Brandon Jørgensen's design creates a zen-like retreat perfectly complementary to the surrounding landscape.

The entrance garden is conceived as a porchlike atrium leading to a solid redwood door that was crafted from the only tree that was removed from the site. This door opens to a small glass foyer, which connects the two main structures of the house. To one side is an interior gateway through a cedar wall, and to the other side is a portal through a thick stone wall. The gateway opens to a garden and guest rooms, and the portal opens to a space occupied by the owners' art collection. The structure then opens to the vineyards on the Napa Valley floor with panoramic views of the Mayacamas Mountains.

The guest rooms through the cedar gateway open to views of the southern vineyards, Stone Mountain, and Mount Veeder. Large eaves provide a place to enjoy the outdoors all year-round with protection from the summer sun.

LEFT: The house was sited so that this magnolia tree is in the sightlines of multiple points within the house.

ABOVE: The entrance of the house is approached from a busy road and so presents a closed facade to maximize privacy.

OPPOSITE: A glass-enclosed entry foyer connects the stone wall of the main house with the wood-and-glass wall of the guesthouse.

ABOVE LEFT: A small aperture faces south from the reading nook.

ABOVE: This entry court is a gentle transition from the closed-off entrance facade to a private, yet open pavilion.

LEFT: A long, serene gallery connects the guesthouse with the living areas of the main house.

OPPOSITE: The living areas of the main house are arranged around a central fireplace.

LEFT: Once opened up, the master bedroom functions as a sleeping porch during warm Napa Valley summer nights.

ABOVE: The central courtyard serves as a point of connection to the various sleeping and living spaces.

NAPA CABIN

OWNERS: Anonymous
ARCHITECT: Luke Wade, Wade Design Architects

When they discovered this location, surrounded on three sides by a state park and overlooking a vineyard, the owners knew this was their "inevitable place." The driveway extends a half mile through the park, and the house emerges from the shaded hillside climb, surrounded on all sides by a mix of redwoods, evergreens, and native deciduous trees. The building site is nestled into the trees and overlooking the vineyard and the ridges of the hillsides beyond.

The owners originally intended to use the structure as a guesthouse, but as they spent more time on the properties (they purchased the land next door for hiking as well as additional privacy), it became evident that the new dwelling was better suited to their lifestyle. The 1,200-square-foot cabin includes a master suite and a great room comprising the kitchen, dining area, living area, and sleeping loft with guest bath. The exterior areas include a spa, an outdoor fireplace, an outdoor kitchen, and a firepit. The design for the great room both saved space and allowed each functional place a sense of intimacy. The dining table became a lovely alcove banquette with tall steel windows and views of the lower vineyard. The kitchen occupies a pantry-like space with a beautiful view. The master bedroom is a sanctuary by any definition. This is a bold flourish of design, materials, and finesse in a rugged environment.

RIGHT: Perched on wooded knoll above the rolling vineyard, the cabin beckons with a lantern-like allure.

LEFT: An outdoor fireplace anchors the wraparound porch and overlooks a garden terrace nestled into the hillside below.

ABOVE: A corten-steel firepit provides a more intimate forest experience among the redwoods near the porch.

RIGHT: The strong central axis of the double-height main room is emphasized by a soaring fireplace flue that slips between timber trusses and into the light monitor above. A library ladder leads to a cozy loft.

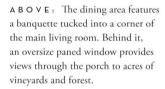

ABOVE: The dining area features a banquette tucked into a corner of the main living room. Behind it, an oversize paned window provides views through the porch to acres of vineyards and forest.

RIGHT: The kitchen provides all necessary amenities within a petite footprint, and is moored by a squarely proportioned island with a custom-designed pot rack above.

ABOVE: A hanging daybed custom designed by Jen Macdonald and handcrafted by Gabe Statsky occupies pride of place at one corner of the wrap around porch.

RIGHT: Views of the distant wooded ridgelines are balanced by the intimate scale of the master bedroom, which opens onto the wraparound porch.

Postscript

"Thank God there is still something on this
planet that belongs completely to the process
and the mysterious and the aesthetic..."

—BIANCA BOSKER, *Cork Dork*

SANTA BARBARA ARTIST'S RESIDENCE

OWNER: Kappy J. Wells

ARCHITECT: Marley + Wells Architects

KAPPY WELLS:

At 69 I am finally living in a Dad house—an earth shelter designed by my architect brother, Sam, and his architect wife, Diana, and inspired by the work of my father, Mac Wells. Due to numerous delays caused by various state and local agencies, the house took almost six years to progress from original concept to finality—although there is no real finality because these things keep evolving. The native chaparrals, with their toyon, chamise, sage, and artemisia—not to mention animals—are slowly returning to claim this area that was once theirs. I'd like to think the house appears welcoming to them.

The steel is rusting, boards are fading, and vines are slowly taking over the concrete. The original site—a sorry-looking spot abandoned by the previous owner after he'd bulldozed into the hillside, leaving a big gouge of crumbling shale the size of a building—was predetermined, before we came along.

All of it, the steel and the wood and the concrete, feel animate to me. There is a feeling of safety and comfort being in and under the earth, timeless and very quiet. Because the house was designed to capture most of the sun's wintry rays, it is perfectly aligned on

RIGHT: North side of the house is tucked into the surrounding natural landscape.

LEFT: The main living space, which includes kitchen, dining, and living areas, opens onto a dramatically framed terrace with ocean views.

a north-south axis, allowing the steel beams to perform as large sundials. It stays cool in the hot months and pleasant in the winter.

A roadrunner comes every afternoon and looks in all of the windows. Hummingbirds click and circle around. Hundreds of quail and lizards scurry by seemingly feeling safe. Coyotes and deer peer in with curiosity from a distance. Buzzards and hawks check it out daily.

I would like to believe that were I to leave, all of this nature (or future humans, of course) would slowly come inside and settle.

Putting aside the scary environmental threats to all of California, I hope this place will have its chance to continue on for many years as a home and sanctuary.

SAM WELLS:

This project is the result of what happens when a sister engages her brother, and his wife, to design a home based on their father's ideas. Simple! Even simpler in that our father was an architect who left us an easy recipe to follow, a recipe that he conceived in the 1960s.

About 55 years ago our father, Malcolm Wells, shifted the focus of this architectural practice to what he came to call "gentle architecture," a method of design that recognized and attempted to embody the lessons that wilderness offers. The most noteworthy result of this method was the deep earth cover that wrapped and topped his projects—as a means to store water, enhance the soil, provide habitat (for more than just humans), and to moderate climate change. Here, in the early twenty-first century, this approach to design is best characterized by the "green roofs" that are ubiquitous on prominent projects around the world.

In 1965, when Mac's first article on the subject of wilderness-based design was published in *Progressive Architecture*, it resulted to letters to the editor, by fellow architects, decrying such ideas. A few years later, with the advent of the first Earth Day, things

started to change. Flash forward another 40 years and green roofs, porous paving, and solar arrays are all part of current code-approval processes.

In 1971 Mac developed his own precursor to today's green codes: a simple evaluation guide with 15 criteria, which he called Absolutely Constant Incontestably Stable Architectural Value Scale. What the scale may have lacked in terms of specific metrics, it handily made up for with its ease of use, and it became the guide for this project. Incidentally, when *Progressive Architecture* published an article on this Value Scale in 1971, the editors claimed "that times have finally caught up with Malcolm Wells."

By incorporating a deep earth cover (basically 200 pounds per square foot of damp earth on the roof) atop this 800 square foot home with accompanying studio, we were able to achieve many of Mac's goals: a building that creates pure air, stores rainwater, creates soils, and uses solar energy—and that achieves a score on the positive side of Mac's Value Scale. By also using only plants native to the site's environmental zone, we hope to reestablish on this site, which had previously been improperly graded, a landscape that can maintain itself. Similarly, our use of exposed concrete, both inside and outside of the structures, will help to lower ongoing maintenance while providing the necessary thermal mass for the project's heating and cooling requirements.

Hopefully, our descendants' descendants will be able to use this project well into the future—such that the final embodied energy of its steel and concrete will well offset the energy used in their initial manufacture. And although our father's first directive would probably have been to do nothing, he was keen on finding what he called "ruined" land and restoring it.

I hope, to some degree, we have.

OPPOSITE: On the south terrace, a battered concrete wall is enlivened by a bronze bas-relief created by the owner.

RIGHT: The property features an artist's studio, which is entered through a door featuring a custom cast-bronze door pull.

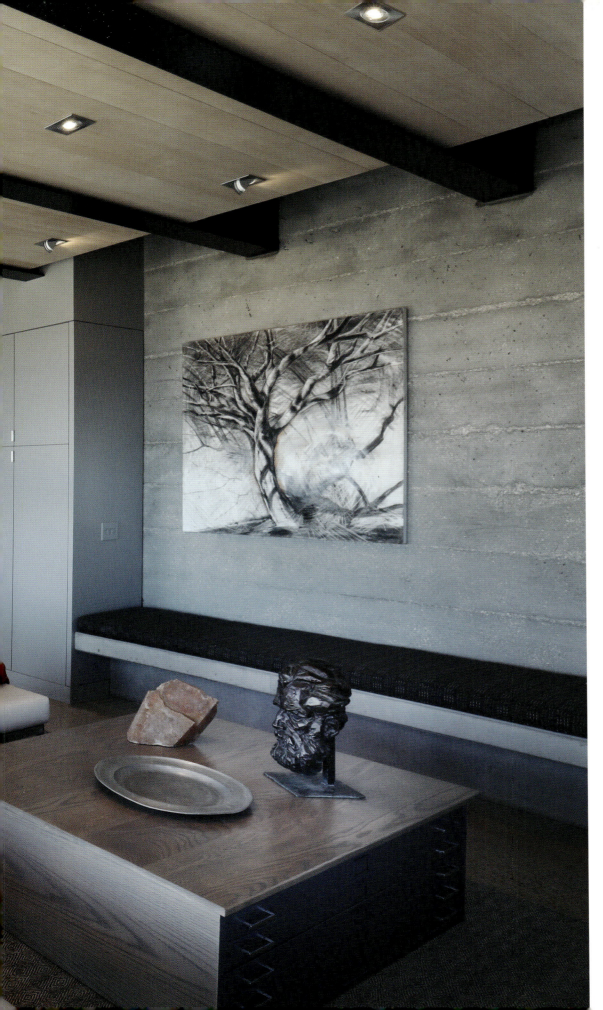

PREVIOUS PAGES: In the main living space, the fireplace is constructed of battered and blasted poured-in-place concrete.

LEFT: The main space containing kitchen, dining, and living areas features exposed steel beams and polished concrete floors.

PHOTOGRAPHY CREDITS

Andréa Johnson: pp. 1, 2, 5, 8, 22, 54, 116, 198, 272

Flying Leap Residence & Liquidity Wines
Peter Powles: pp. 10–11, 14–15
John Adrian: pp. 12, 13, 16, 17, 18–19, 20–21

Cole Farmhouse and Schoolhouse
Paul Dyer: pp. 24–25, 26–27, 28, 29, 30–31, 32–33, 34, 35

Jørgensen Residence
Joe Fletcher/OTTO: pp. 36–37, 38, 39, 40–41, 42–43, 44, 45

Telesis 2.0
Joe Fletcher: pp. 46–47, 48, 49, 50, 51, 52, 53

Lovall Valley
Peter Vivianis: pp. 56–57
Rebecca Kmiec: pp. 58, 59, 60–61, 62, 63, 64–65

Sonoma Coast Vineyard Residence
Art Grice: pp. 66–67, 68, 69, 70, 71, 72, 73

Dry Creek Residence
Blake Marvin: pp. 74–75, 76, 77, 78–79, 80–81, 82, 83

Sonoma Vineyard Estate
John Sutton: pp. 84–85, 86, 87, 88, 89, 90, 91, 92, 93

Lucunda Vineyard Residence
Marion Brenner: pp. 94–95, 97 bottom, 98, 99, 100–1
Russell Abraham: 96, 97 top

Iron Horse Vineyards
John Dimaio: pp. 102–3, 104, 105, 106–7

Sonoma Hillside House
Rebecca Kmiec: pp. 108–9, 110, 111, 112, 113, 114, 115

Naramata Bench House
Ema Peter: pp. 118–19, 120, 121, 122, 123, 124, 125, 126, 127

Sequitur Vineyard
Jeremy Bitterman: pp. 128–29, 130, 131, 132, 133, 134, 135

Tasting Room, Sokol Blosser Winery & Vineyards
Jeremy Bitterman: pp. 136–37, 138, 139, 140–41

Canopy & Glass House
Paul Warchol: pp. 144–45, 146–47, 148–49, 150, 151, 152, 153

Novelty Hill-Januik Winery
Ben Benschneider: pp. 154–55, 156, 157

Weathering Seattle House
Paul Warchol: pp. 158–59, 160, 161, 162–63, 164, 165, 166, 167

South Okanagan House
Martin Knowles: pp. 168–69, 170, 171, 172, 173

Martin's Lane Winery
Nic Lehoux: pp. 174–75, 176, 177, 178, 179

Red Mountain Vineyard Residence
Andrew Pogue: pp. 180–81, 182, 183, 184, 185, 186, 187

Santa Lucia Preserve
Joe Fletcher/OTTO: pp. 188–89, 190, 191, 192, 193, 194, 195, 196, 197

Sentinel Ridge Vineyard Residence
Matthew Millman: pp. 200–1, 202, 203, 204–5, 206, 207, 208, 209

Rutherford Vineyard Residence
Sam Frost: pp. 214, 218, 219 bottom
Tim Griffith: pp. 210–11, 212–13, 215, 216–17, 219 top

James Cole Estate Winery
John Dimaio: pp. 220–21, 222, 223, 224, 225

Zinfandel Vineyards Residence
Joe Fletcher: pp. 226–27, 228, 229, 230, 231, 232, 233

Macayamas Mountain Residence
Scott Frances/OTTO: pp. 234–35, 236, 237, 238, 239, 240, 241, 242, 243

Oak Knoll Vineyard Residence
Russell Abraham: pp. 244–45, 246, 247, 248–49, 250, 251, 252, 253

Oak Knoll District Residence
Joe Fletcher/OTTO: pp. 254–55, 256, 257, 258, 259, 260, 261, 262, 263

Napa Cabin
Paul Dyer: pp. 264–65, 266, 267, 268, 269, 270, 271

Santa Barbara Artist's Residence
John Dimaio: pp. 274–75, 276–77, 278, 279, 280–81, 282–83

ACKNOWLEDGMENTS

Thank you to the generous owners and the winemakers, those whose homes and vineyards offer us an invigorating look at the celebratory side of a radically disconnected and exhaustive existence. My appreciation also to the architects whose structures integrate the character and voice of the surrounding land. To the photographers, your brilliant work is an honor to publish. Thank you.

The notes, books, and stories that composed the research for this book led to the discovery of a curious aura attached to the title of the book. It may be a cloying cliché for those who live in regions where vineyards are planted and wine is conjured by ritual magic, but the fact is one can never forget that one is in wine country. The locations featured here include Santa Barbara in California as the most southern location, then moving north through Oregon and Washington to the Naramata Bench in the Okanagan of British Columbia, Canada. The structures are set in zen-like, soft, hilly lands with small gatherings of pretty deer, and their designs reflect mid-century classicism, with its deep archival design enthusiasms, or Corten steel in vertical or angled or horizontal planes—a brash show of geometric confidence. There is an intimate house on a pond and an earth shelter house that is an architectural family affair. None of these descriptions speak directly of wine; nevertheless, the aura is ever present and without a doubt a tasting room, a vineyard, or winery is close enough to fill the glass you may have in your hand.

On this expedition I have had the great good fortune to work with the force that fights primarily for the land—an army of conscientious humans who are the first protectors of the fields and hills and waterways. With absolute certainty their work, their land, and the surrounding lands and water sources are maintained under careful, proactive, and continuous cultivation. These growers may appear to be a small corps, but every continent, country, county, and suburb on earth has its prime valleys, foothills, mountainsides, glacial paths, savannas, and foggy coastal plains planted with grapevines. This global corps of grape-growers and winemakers are the grape-earth-sky bodhisattvas. Here's to them.

I would like to thank Hayley Blomquist of Artists Rights Society for her expertise in managing the licensing of rights and permissions for the publication of Alexander Calder's paintings. I am grateful to the Calder Foundation for their kind generosity and permissions. Thanks to Brandon Jørgensen Atelier; Joy Sterling, CEO of Iron Horse Vineyards; Jess Field at FIELD Architecture; Colleen Redfield at Cutler Anderson Architects; Lisa Smedley at Sagan Piechota Architecture; Rebecca Kmiec for her photography and as liaison to Conrad/Asturi Design; Joel Sanders of the Joel B. Sanders Agency; Melissa Le Boeuf at the OTTO Agency; Colleen Harder of The James Cole Winery; and Jerry Judkins-Smith of Inland Desert Nursery.

I am profoundly grateful to have worked with Rizzoli International Publications on 15 books. Charles Miers, president and publisher of Rizzoli, has been an inspiration, psychiatrist, and always a tower of strength. Thank you, Charles. My praise for graphic designer Lynne Yeamans is a joy. Her quixotic pragmatism is emotional; from cover to cover, her layouts make me smile. My thanks to you once again, Lynne.

ABOVE: Panaoramic view of the
approach to Iron Horse Vineyards.